Christ and the Spirit presents an accessible entry t[...] [...] the [...]
ples from contemporary culture to demonstrate [...] [...] of the [...] and in the
world. The book's concise explanations of theological principles and their applications
complement its detailed rendition of the way Jesus Christ is presented in Scripture and
received through the ages.

—Phyllis Zagano
Hofstra University

Christ and the Spirit provides a well-researched and accessible overview of Catholic
perspectives on Jesus Christ and the Holy Spirit from a Western, Catholic, Christian
understanding as they have emerged and developed over the past two millennia. What is
innovative about Markey's approach is his exploration of these traditions through story
and film. Using the films *Beauty and the Beast* and *Star Wars*, and with input by colleague Greg Zuschlag, Markey explores the meaning and significance of the Christ and
the Holy Spirit through the lens, particularly, of Belle (Beauty) as a "Christ-figure," one
who saves as Christ does humanity from sin and death. This approach forces readers to
rethink their understanding of Jesus for today.

The book is well written, engaging, and thought provoking. I highly recommend
it as especially appealing for use in undergraduate and graduate theology and religious
studies courses. This small book (students will appreciate the brevity), opens up new ways
of thinking about and understanding Jesus Christ for the twenty-first century.

—Diana L. Hayes
Georgetown University

Christ and the Spirit offers a remarkably thorough survey of major historical developments in the understanding of Jesus Christ and the Holy Spirit. It is both a compelling
tour of the theological concerns and questions that gave rise to those developments and a
creative exploration of how the Christian community's insights might continue to make
a claim on us today. John Markey has provided a book that will delight teachers and
students alike. He and his colleague, Greg Zuschlag, are master teachers, inviting their
readers to think with depth and precision about the transformative work of Jesus Christ
and the Spirit in our world.

—Steve Rodenborn
St. Edward's University

"Imagining the world or one's life differently is the first step in changing it." So states
John Markey in his introduction to *Christ and the Spirit: Catholic Perspectives through the
Ages*. Convinced that people must access God through their own experience if they are to
authentically connect to the God of Christianity, and equally convinced of the epistemo-
logical power of story, Markey, along with contributor Greg Zuschlag, lace a lucid outline
of Western Christianity's theologies of Christ and the Spirit with illustrations from the
film narratives of *Beauty and the Beast*, *Superman*, and *Star Wars*. In the case of *Beauty
and the Beast*, he illuminates the ways in which the story's heroine, Belle, functions as a
Christ figure, returning to her again and again in reflection question boxes that challenge
readers to make their own connections and draw their own conclusions on the basis of
his elaboration of the developments of the Christian Tradition. In evoking *Superman* and
Star Wars, he acknowledges popular parallels, respectively, to Christ and the Spirit, but

counsels caution and invites critical analysis vis-à-vis an authentic understanding of the paschal mystery. Both his boxed reflections and discussion questions lead the reader to recognize the truth-in-contrast between the redemptive power of Belle's vulnerable love and the myth of redemptive violence perpetuated by Superman and the Force. Recurring references to Jean Vanier's L'Arche communities reinforce the vision of the world through the lens of the Christian story that Markey so successfully conveys.

This book is a rich resource for undergraduate introductory courses as well as for continuing formation for adults. It provides excellent pedagogical tools for the classroom and for popular pastoral education.

—Kathleen McManus, OP
University of Portland

What a well-informed, concise, and imaginative book this is! John Markey's *Christ and the Spirit* signals a promising direction in response to Jesus' enduring question: Who do you say that I am? Markey recognizes that a genuine answer to this question requires the active presence of the Spirit of Jesus, the Holy Spirit. Well-chosen films with prominent Christ-figures invite readers to consider God's wondrous and surprising presence among us and the ways in which the Spirit transforms and empowers us. Throughout, this book remains faithful to the best biblical and theological work of our time.

—Nancy Pineda-Madrid
Boston College

This refreshing and highly accessible work purports to offer a logical and creative analysis of the testimony of the Christian Scriptures as well as two millennia of Christian thinking about Jesus Christ, the visible image of the invisible God and the Spirit who reveals him.

Because of its faithfulness to the sources of Christianity as well as a creative use of familiar images from contemporary literature and film, *Christ and the Spirit* invites its readers to think more clearly about their experience and interpretation of God's presence in their lives and history, and how that experience might (or might not) connect with the Christian experience of God acting in Jesus Christ and the Holy Spirit. After presenting the saving mystery, the book has the courage to ask "so what?"—hoping to help the reader come to know something new and significant about the Christian understanding of God's love made present to human beings through Jesus Christ and the Spirit.

This book has valuable insights for college students and participants in programs of adult faith formation. I highly recommend it.

—Cardinal Joseph W. Tobin, C.Ss.R.
Archbishop of Newark

Christ and the Spirit

Catholic Perspectives through the Ages

John J. Markey

Author Acknowledgments

I would like to acknowledge and thank Greg Zuschlag for his friendship, advice, and invaluable contributions to this small book. I would like to acknowledge the outstanding and dedicated work of my research assistant, Joseph August Higgins, and his contributions developing the content of this book. I am deeply grateful for the hospitality, generosity, and love of Cyd Crouse and Niels Caminada, Rob and Charlie Streit, and my mother, Sharron Markey. I am grateful for the encouragement, insights, and support of my friends Rose Chalifoux, Jake Hebbert, Theresa Galan-Bruce, Lynn Streit, my colleagues at Oblate School of the Theology, and my Dominican brothers of the Province of St. Martin De Porres. Finally, I am indebted to Brad Harmon, Paul Peterson, and especially Maura Thompson Hagarty at Anselm Academic for their support, advice, companionship, and trust.

Publisher Acknowledgments

Thank you to the following individuals who reviewed this work in progress:

Brian Doyle, *Marymount University, Arlington, VA*
Elena Procario-Foley, *Iona College, New Rochelle, NY*
Shannon Schrein, OSF, *Lourdes University, Sylvania, OH*

Created by the publishing team of Anselm Academic.

The scriptural quotations in this book are from the *New American Bible, revised edition* © 2010, 1991, 1986, and 1970 by the Confraternity of Christian Doctrine, Inc., Washington, DC. Used by permission of the copyright owner. All rights reserved. No part of this work may be reproduced in any form without permission in writing from the copyright owner.

Cover image: Image in Public Domain

Printed in the United States of America

7085

ISBN 978-1-59982-952-4

Dedication

Patricia Bruno, OP

Jude Siciliano, OP

Friends and mentors

Contents

Introduction

While religious practice and affiliation has decreased drastically over the last twenty years, interest in spirituality and God has increased. The US cultural context is one of the most religiously engaged on earth. But basic questions remain about God, the meaning and purpose of life, and the possibilities of hope and love and of changing the world for the better. The Catholic Christian tradition offers thoughtful, complex, and compelling responses to such questions, but it's message is often obscured by negative images, limited and even false explanations, and the hypocritical divide between the life and action of some Catholics.

This book attempts to set out clearly the Catholic tradition regarding Jesus Christ and the Holy Spirit. It also attempts to address readers' questions: "So what?" "What difference does this make?" "How can I imagine these realities working in the lives of individuals and communities today?" "How does the tradition help illuminate and clarify contemporary experiences of God? What is the relationship between this tradition and my own spiritual journey?" It is hoped that readers will gain a good understanding of the Catholic tradition and an awareness that there are many strands in that tradition. It is also hoped that readers will come to appreciate how some of those strands might contribute to their personal religious perspectives.

A Theology of Jesus Christ

In one sense, this book is not really about Jesus of Nazareth. It does not offer a new perspective on his life or historical context nor does it analyze his sayings or message in any detail. This book does not attempt a Christology "from below," that is, developing a theological interpretation of the Jesus of history primarily through interpreting Jesus' life, actions, and teachings as described in the Gospels. Nor is it merely a Christology from above, that is, an abstract theology of the "Christ of faith" as relayed in certain New Testament texts and the Western theological tradition. In fact, this account finds both approaches inadequate.

Rather, the goal of this short book is to lay out in a clear, comprehensive, and accessible manner the central ideas and key developments in the understanding of Jesus Christ (Christology) in the Western Christian theological tradition. Although this study comes out of the Catholic perspective, it remains open to other perspectives and divergent interpretations within the Catholic tradition. For this reason, it focuses on the theological interpretation of the life, death, and Resurrection of Jesus Christ by both the writers of the New Testament[1] and the Christian theological tradition. The New Testament serves primarily as theological interpretation of the action of God in Jesus and the Holy Spirit and as such is the foundation of all subsequent theology in the Christian tradition. *Tradition* refers to an ongoing process of interpretation and renewal as theologians have reinterpreted and reappropriated the New Testament witness in ways that made sense to the people of their cultural and historical contexts. In each generation and each cultural location, Christians must respond anew to Jesus' question, "Who do you say that I am?" (Matt. 16:15). That is, they must attempt to answer their own questions about the identity, meaning, and purpose of Jesus Christ. This book attempts to relay the major movements in this Christological tradition and demonstrate how they both develop and retain the truth about God and Jesus as revealed in the New Testament.

A Theology of the Holy Spirit

The New Testament narrates and reflects upon the story of Jesus Christ and the Holy Spirit. Both act in integral and interconnected ways throughout the Gospels and the early Christian community's interpretation of the presence of God in their lives and history. Furthermore, the whole of Scripture (both the Old and New Testaments) depicts God as fundamentally present and active in the world. In the New Testament, God is particularly portrayed as transforming individuals and communities through the action of the Spirit. It is important, therefore, to look carefully at the role, function, and understanding of the Spirit in order to understand Jesus Christ, and vice versa. This book attempts to offer a basic analysis of the Spirit as presented in the New Testament. This analysis necessarily includes both the Spirit's relationship to Jesus and the Spirit's identity as the presence of God in human lives. This study also explores the emergence of

---

1. Christians view the Bible as a two-volume work consisting of the Old and New Testaments. In conveying their interpretation of Jesus, the writers of the New Testament tend to use images, characters, stories, and texts from the Old Testament, a collection of sacred texts of the Jewish faith. The writers of the New Testament transformed the meaning and purpose of these texts. They also created their own, new Scripture, the New Testament, which does not replace or reject the Old Testament but elaborates on it and brings it to fulfilment from a Christian point of view. See further Luke Timothy Johnson, *The Writings of the New Testament*, 3rd ed. (Minneapolis: Fortress, 2010), 129–33.

a distinctive theology of the Holy Spirit (pneumatology) in the early theological tradition, the challenges and shortcomings of this tradition in the history of Western theology, and the renewed interest in and development of pneumatology in the modern and contemporary periods. In conclusion, it offers some fundamental insights on the person and action of the Spirit and the foundational role of pneumatology for all aspects of theological reflection.

Exploring Christ and the Spirit through Story and Film

This book attempts to set out a Western, Catholic, Christian understanding of Jesus Christ and the Holy Spirit. As such, its goal is to do theology through a variety of modes, employing both rational and intuitive or pre-rational means to explore a Christian interpretation of God's actions in human lives. This study is synthetic in that it tries to bring together traditional Christian theology with some creative and artistic attempts to make sense of the meaning and purpose of human life and the ways that humans can be changed and transformed by love and hope. By combining rational theology with a famous fairy-tale or fable (and now a movie) and other iconic images, the authors seek to offer an exploration of some of the major themes that emerge out of Christology and pneumatology. Chapter 1 includes analysis of the famous fairy-tale "Beauty and the Beast" as it has been told in story, stage, and film over hundreds of years. The author of this section, Greg Zuschlag, explores the meaning of the story and the ways in which its heroine, Belle (the "beauty"), can help deepen an investigation of the person and mission of Jesus Christ. The author contends that Belle represents a remarkable example of a "Christ-figure" in literature and one of the best examples of the Christian understanding of how Christ saves or redeems human beings from sin and death. Each chapter invites the reader to consider the ways in which this fable can shed light on the theology of Jesus Christ. In chapter 2, contributing author Greg Zuschlag, contrasts Belle as heroine and savior with another iconic cultural hero: Superman. In the third chapter, the role of Belle is similarly compared to that of another important cultural icon: the idea of "the force" from the Star Wars movies.

This study does not investigate every possible interpretation of God's activity offered in Scripture or the Western Catholic Christian tradition. Rather, it aims to help students to think about and interpret more clearly their experience of God's presence in their lives and history and how that experience might or might not connect with the Christian experience of God acting in Jesus Christ and the Holy Spirit. Understanding often comes when people connect their experience with some wider human experience told as a story. Making sense of the world requires both rational knowledge and creative insights that enable people to grasp truth and meaning for themselves. Imagining the world or one's life differently is the first step toward effecting change. What follows is thus a logical and creative analysis aimed at helping the reader come to know something new and significant about the Christian understanding of God's love made present to human beings through Jesus Christ and the Spirit.

Jesus Christ: New Testament Perspectives

L
ike all of Christian theology, the theology of Jesus Christ (Christology) is rooted in the Scriptures. It is said that Jesus came to talk about the reign of God and the first Christians were primarily interested in talking about Jesus;[1] the New Testament talks about both. The New Testament texts all agree that in some way Jesus of Nazareth embodies his fundamental message and revelation that God is love. But the texts each also offer something unique about Jesus, both in their method of interpreting him and in the themes they develop. This chapter examines what the Christian Scriptures reveal about Jesus Christ as the Second Person of the Trinity, his relationship and identification with the Father and the Spirit, the purpose for which he comes to participate in human history, and how his identity affects the lives and destiny of all human beings.

---

1. The reign of God, also called the "kingdom of God" or the "dominion of God" (from the Greek *basileia tou Theou*), is a central theme in the Gospels and shaped the earliest Christian community's understanding of the significance and identity of Jesus as the Son of God. For a textual analysis of the theme of the reign of God in the Gospels, see N. T. Wright, *Christian Origins and the Question of God*, vol. 2, *Jesus and the Victory of God*, 1st North American ed. (Minneapolis: Fortress, 1992), 443–51; Raymond E. Brown, *An Introduction to New Testament Christology* (New York: Paulist Press, 1994), 60–70; and Ben Witherington III, *The Christology of Jesus* (Minneapolis: Fortress, 1990), 191–206. For an attempt at a systematic analysis of the meaning of the reign of God in the New Testament, see Edward Schillebeeckx, trans. Hubert Hoskins, *Jesus and Experiment in Christology* (New York: Crossroad, 1989). For an analysis of the significance of the message of the reign of God from the earliest Christian communities after Jesus' death and subsequent Resurrection and its continued significance today, see Jurgen Moltmann, *The Crucified God: The Cross of Christ as the Foundation and Criticism of Christian Theology* (Minneapolis: Fortress, 1993); Jurgen Moltmann, *The Coming of God: Christian Eschatology* (Minneapolis: Fortress, 2004); Edward Schillebeeckx, trans. Hubert Hoskins, *Jesus: An Experiment in Christology* (New York: Crossroads, 1989); and Edward Schillebeeckx, trans. John Bowden, *Christ: The Experience of Jesus as Lord* (New York: Crossroad, 1989).

The Identity of Jesus Christ in the Christian Scriptures

The sections of the New Testament offering the most significant contribution to Christology are the four Gospels and the letters (or epistles) attributed to Paul. For brevity's sake, the following discussion is limited to these works.

The four Gospels all tell the story of the life, teachings, and significant events of the historical person Jesus of Nazareth.[2] The Gospels agree that Jesus and his followers were faithful Jews who understood their whole lives in terms Jewish religious life and the Jewish Scriptures. The Gospels also agree that the story of Jesus' life and ministry culminates in his betrayal, trial, torture, and death at the hands of both the Jewish and Roman authorities. Likewise, the Gospels all attest to his Resurrection from the dead and his promise that he will come again to redeem and restore all of creation according God's plan. Specific Gospels also discuss Jesus' gift of his Spirit upon his followers and his return (Ascension) to his place in God's own life. The paschal mystery—Jesus' suffering, death, Resurrection, and giving of his Spirit to the community—comprise the central event for the Gospel authors and the Apostle Paul. For Catholic Christians, Jesus Christ revealed the inner mystery and ultimate plan of God. In this chapter, it should become clear that for the early Christians (and the subsequent tradition) this mystery reveals the identity of Jesus Christ and through him the true mystery and destiny of every human life.

The paschal mystery serves as the starting point and the central theme for the whole of the New Testament. The texts of the New Testament, therefore, primarily attempt to shed light on this mystery and to understand its implications for diverse communities of Christians who held it as their foundation and common point of reference. The Gospels, in particular, attempt to interpret the paschal mystery in terms of the life and preaching of Jesus of Nazareth. In telling the story of Jesus, they try to tell the story of God's action in and through him and to make sense of his death and Resurrection, which they see as the culmination and vindication of his life and mission. The epistles, on the other hand (especially the letters of Paul), often focus upon the practical implications of following Jesus through faith for ordinary Christians and their communities. They also often reflect theologically on the Christian understanding of Jesus himself and his unique revelation about the inner life and remarkable nature of God.

The New Testament authors wrote for those who believed they had already encountered the risen Christ and embraced the mystery of God that this encounter entailed. Both the Gospels and the epistles challenge converted Christians

---

2. See further Luke Timothy Johnson, *The Writings of the New Testament*, 3rd ed. (Minneapolis: Fortress, 2010), 129–33.

to deepen their faith in the God that is revealed by Jesus Christ. The epistles are primarily intended to help these early communities develop into the image of Christ (Col. 3:9–11) and to take on "the same attitude that is also yours in Christ Jesus" (Phil. 2:5). The Gospels are intended to help Christians to grow in the task of genuine discipleship: following Jesus. Faith in Jesus implies there will be critical moments in the lives of believers when they should reaffirm, deepen, and act upon their fundamental confidence that Jesus Christ represented God in a unique and authoritative way. Christians therefore are the primary audience that the texts of the New Testament seek to inform, enable, and inspire.

The Gospels

The four Gospels, Matthew, Mark, Luke, and John, provide four distinct yet interrelated accounts of the life, death, and Resurrection of Jesus of Nazareth as well as a collection of his spiritual and moral teachings. Like the rest of the New Testament, the Gospels were written in Greek toward the end of the first century CE. Mark was most likely written first (ca. 60–75), probably deriving from a combination of oral and written traditions from the earliest Christian communities in Rome. Matthew was likely written next (ca. 70–100), probably in Syria or northern Palestine, to a largely Gentile audience that would have been familiar with Jewish history and traditions. Third to be written was likely Luke (ca. 75–95), which probably originated in Palestine with a Gentile audience in mind, similar to Matthew's Gospel. As the first part of a two-volume work (the Acts of the Apostles is the second part), Luke attempts to take the received oral and written traditions available to him and provide an "orderly" account (Luke 1:2–3). Last of all was the Gospel of John (ca. 80–110). Like Mark, and unlike Matthew and Luke, the Gospel of John was likely written outside of Palestine. It may have originated in either Ephesus or Antioch (in modern-day Turkey), or in Alexandria, Egypt. In either case, John was written in a Greco-Roman context for a largely Greek audience.

Matthew, Mark, and Luke, commonly referred to as the "Synoptic" Gospels (meaning "seeing together" in Greek) share a great deal of material. For example, as much as 95 percent of the verses in Mark also appear in either Matthew or Luke. In contrast, only about 10 percent of the Gospel of John is shared with the other three Gospels.[3]

---

3. The issues of the date and composition of the four Gospels and their relation to each other are complicated and continue to be debated. As David L. Dungan helpfully suggests, ultimately what is at stake here are four interrelated issues that face contemporary readers of the

The Four Gospels

The word "gospel" derives from the Old English words *god* (meaning "God" or "good") and *spell* (meaning "news" or "story"). "Gospel" translates the Greek word *euangelion*, which means "good news." In the Gospels, Jesus announces that his fundamental mission is to bring humanity "good news" by proclaiming and offering an example of the reign of God: "He has anointed me to bring glad tidings to the poor . . . to proclaim liberty to the captives" (Luke 4:18; see also Isa. 61:1). In many ways, Jesus follows in the line of the Old Testament prophets by proclaiming the love and mercy of God and urging people to turn away from a life of sin and selfishness and toward a new life of salvation marked by love toward God and selflessness toward others. What is new is that Jesus claims to have a unique relationship to the reign of God in that he is already living in God's reign and is bringing it into people's lives. The willingness of those who encounter Jesus to follow his example and accept his teaching is a sign of the presence of the reign of God. In other words, Jesus' life and ministry embody the power of God's presence and the living reality of God's salvation. More about Jesus' personal identification with the reign of God in each Gospel is discussed below.

The Gospels are written as stories that narrate the message of and the critical events in the life of Jesus as well as help interpret the meaning of those teachings and events for the author's community or communities. The narrative method is extremely effective in helping Christian communities imagine and identify with Jesus as a human person like themselves and to put themselves into the story so they can better see how to incorporate his story into their own lives. The Gospel writers act as theologians who are engaged in theological reflection through a narrative method. These theologians are not historians or journalists, but neither are they artists writing fiction to entertain. Telling stories is an effective and ancient form of communication for passing on the accumulated wisdom of the community, especially in cultures in which most people cannot read or write. So it is important to treat the Gospels as theology and their writers as theologians. It is also important to remember that in the Christian view even today believers write gospels, in the sense that each community narrates its own Spirit-inspired accounts of Jesus' life, death, and Resurrection in the light of its new and unique situation. These accounts will necessarily be selective, biased, and partial, based on the needs and challenges

---

Gospels: (1) Which Gospel should I consult? (2) Which text(s) of that Gospel should I use? (3) What should I know about the creation of this Gospel? (4) How can I faithfully interpret the text's meaning for today? By situating questions about the interrelations of the Synoptic Gospels in relation to questions about how to interpret the Bible faithfully, biblical scholars highlight the value of having four different yet related accounts of Jesus' earthly ministry. See David L. Dungan, *A History of the Synoptic Problem: The Canon, the Text, the Composition, and the Interpretation of the Gospels*, 1st ed., Anchor Bible (New York: Doubleday, 1999), 349–67.

facing a community at a particular time. The twentieth-century Catholic theologian Edward Schillebeeckx claimed that all Christian communities are called to create a "fifth gospel"—indeed, to become a "fifth gospel"—to reinterpret and enliven the basic story in their shared life.[4]

CHRIST-FIGURES IN FILM

Exploring *Beauty and the Beast*

Greg Zuschlag[5]

Most people are familiar with the story *Beauty and the Beast*. It has been told and retold endlessly in children's books and films. It has also been analyzed by psychologists, sociologists, and feminist literary critics. The tale admits to as many interpretations as there are versions of the story. Thus, while the story is well known, what exactly it is about and what it means is open to interpretation. It is considered a great work of literature in that, like a "never-ending artichoke," it contains "the possibility of being able to continue to unpeel, discovering more and more new dimensions."[6]

© Walt Disney Pictures / courtesy Everett Collection

This brief study considers this beloved fairy tale from a Christological point of view. Admittedly, there is nothing intentionally or explicitly Christian about the story. When viewed through a Christological lens,

Belle and the Beast from *Beauty and the Beast*

however, *Beauty and the Beast* can shed light on the story of Jesus Christ as presented in the New Testament, a story that demonstrates how the

Continued

---

4. See further Robert J. Schreiter and Mary Catherine Hilkert, eds., *The Praxis of Christian Experience: An Introduction to the Theology of Edward Schillebeeckx* (San Francisco: Harper & Row, 1989), 51; Edward Schillebeeckx, *Church: The Human Story of God*, trans. John Bowden (New York: Crossroad, 1990) 154–57.

5. Greg Zuschlag is Associate Professor of Systematic Theology at Oblate School of Theology, San Antonio, Texas.

6. Jerry Griswold, quoting Italo Calvino in *The Meaning of "Beauty and the Beast": A Handbook* (Ontario, Canada: Broadview, 2004).

power of love redeems a sinful humanity. In this analysis, Belle (French for "Beauty") functions as a Christ-figure whose love restores the humanity of the ugly beast and creates a life-giving and mutually loving relationship between the two. In the Incarnation, as discussed in chapter 2, Jesus Christ embodies God's love for human beings, and that love saves them. That idea is echoed in the oft-quoted phrase by the Russian novelist Fyodor Dostoevsky, "Beauty will save the world," for, as Saint Augustine observed, "Beauty rouses our love; we love what is beautiful."[7]

Plot Summary

Though the "template" for the many adaptations and retellings of the story come from Jeanne-Marie Leprince de Beaumont's 1756 version for nursery-age children in England, this discussion focuses on the way the story is presented in two Disney movies: the 1991 animated musical version (the first animated film ever to receive a nomination for Best Picture from the Academy Awards) and the 2017 live action remake.[8]

The Disney version opens in the castle of a spoiled and heartless young prince. The prince turns away an old beggar, scorning her paltry offer of a rose in exchange for shelter. The beggar then reveals herself as a beautiful enchantress, who turns the prince into a hideous beast. She also turns all the castle's servants into household objects, and enchants the nearby villagers, causing them to forget all about the castle and its inhabitants. The curse could be broken if the prince could learn to love another and earn the love of another before the last petal of the enchantress's rose falls. If he should fail, he and the others would be doomed to remain under the curse forever.

In the nearby village lives Belle, an attractive young woman with an eccentric inventor father. The villagers admire her beauty but consider her odd because she loves books and rejects the advances of Gaston, the handsome but narcissistic young hunter. One day, Belle's dotty father prepares to travel to a distant market. When he asks Belle if he can bring her anything back, she asks for a rose, an expression of her love of simple things. When the father loses his way in the woods, he seeks refuge in the

Continued

---

7. Both quotes are paraphrases by Gerald O'Collins in his book *Christology: A Biblical, Historical, and Systematic Study of Jesus* (Oxford: Oxford University Press, 2009).

8. The plot summary provided here blends the 1991 and 2017 versions for the sake of simplicity.

beast's mysterious castle and is captured by the beast. Belle goes in search of her father and finds him imprisoned in the castle. She asks the beast to allow her to take his place. The beast, somewhat taken aback by this selfless act, agrees: he releases the father and keeps Belle. Belle and the beast gradually begin to see each other in a positive light, and even begin to fall in love.

Then Belle learns that her father is in trouble; Gaston plans to have him locked up in an asylum for the wild story he has been telling the villagers about the beast who is holding his daughter captive in an enchanted castle. The beast, moved by a newfound sense of selflessness, frees Belle so that she may go to the aid her father. On her return, Belle manages to convince the villagers that her father is not crazy and that the beast is real. Gaston, however, whips the villagers into a frenzy of fear and hate, and leads them to the castle to destroy the beast.

The climax of the film finds the beast and Gaston locked in mortal combat on the parapets of the castle. The beast overpowers Gaston, but refuses to kill him, declaring, "I am not a beast!" But as he turns away, Gaston mortally wounds him, though Gaston falls to his death in the process. Belle comes to the beast as he lies dying and declares her love for him. At that moment, as the last rose petal falls, the curse is lifted: the beast is transformed back into a prince and brought back to life, the servants are transformed from being objects to being humans, the castle is restored to its glory, and the townspeople's memory returns. In the end all are reunited at the castle in a joyous scene of dancing in the grand ballroom, the place where the curse began and the place where Belle and the beast's love for one another first flowered, thus bringing a true "happily ever after" ending to this beloved fairy tale.

Beneath the Surface: Theological Analysis

Belle, in *Beauty and the Beast*, can be seen as a Christ-figure. A Christ-figure should not be confused with a "Jesus figure," a person whose words or actions correspond directly to that of Jesus of Nazareth as understood historically or presented in the New Testament. Lloyd Baugh, a Jesuit priest and professor of Theology and Film Studies, explains,

> The Christ-figure is neither Jesus nor the Christ, but rather a shadow, a faint glimmer of reflection of him. As a fully human being, the Christ-figure may be weak, uncertain, even a sinner,

Continued

CHRIST-FIGURES IN FILM: EXPLORING *BEAUTY AND THE BEAST* Continued

that may have all the limitations of any human being in the situation at hand. The Christ-figure is a foil to Jesus Christ, and between the two figures there is a reciprocal relationship. On the one hand, the reference to Christ clarifies the situation of the Christ-figure and adds depth to the significance of his [sic] action; on the other hand, the person and situation of the Christ-figure can provide new understanding of who and how Christ is: Jesus himself is revealed anew in the Christ-figure.[9]

How is Belle a Christ-figure? How does she "reveal anew" how we understand who Jesus is? In particular, what role does beauty play in this analogy?

Several prominent Christian theologians over the centuries have asserted that God is not just truth and goodness but beauty. Saint Augustine actually addresses God as such: "Late have I loved Thee, O Beauty so ancient and so new; late have I loved Thee!"[10] Jonathan Edwards, the American Puritan theologian, focuses on beauty as the principle attribute of God: "God is God, and distinguished from all other beings, and exalted above 'em, chiefly by his divine beauty, which is infinitely diverse from all other beauty."[11]

As Augustine observes, Jesus Christ is not only "beautiful in the hands of his parents" and "beautiful in his miracles" but he is also "beautiful in his flagellation, beautiful giving up his spirit, beautiful carrying the cross, beautiful on the cross, [and] beautiful in heaven."[12] Thus Jesus is paradoxically yet preeminently beautiful in his Crucifixion. Drawing upon the ideas of two twentieth-century theologians, Karl Barth and Hans Urs Von Balthasar, T. Chris Cain comments that "the cross [is] a serendipitous manifestation of the beauty of Christ. The cross, isolated in and of itself, may be viewed as an ugly murder of an innocent man, but when seen in its cosmic scope and in all of its ramifications it is a

Continued

---

9. Lloyd Baugh, *Imaging the Divine: Jesus and Christ-Figures in Film* (Kansas City, MO: Sheed and Ward, 1997), 112.

10. Augustine, *The Confessions of St. Augustine,* trans. F. J. Sheed (New York: Sheed & Ward, 1943), 10.27.

11. Jonathan Edwards, *Treatise on the Religious Affections* (1764), in *The Works of Jonathan Edwards,* vol. 2, *Religious Affections,* ed. John Smith (New Haven: Yale University, 2009), 298.

12. Augustine, *Ennarations on the Psalms,* Psalm 45, as quoted by Richard Villadesau in "*Theosis and Beauty,*" *Theology Today* 65 (2008): 187.

beautiful act. God's hidden beauty is revealed as Christ overcomes the ugliness of sin on the cross."[13]

These observations about the beauty of God and the beauty of Jesus Christ and his Crucifixion help explain how Belle serves as a Christ-figure by loving the ugly beast with a genuine beauty that elicits love, thus lifting the curse of sin in the fairy tale. Belle's beauty appears in multiple ways throughout the film: her deep love for learning and invention; the simplicity of her desire for a rose and not more lavish material goods; her willingness to take her father's place as the prisoner of the beast (an act that confounds the beast); her willingness to look past not just the beast's physical appearance but his spiritual ugliness (his self-centeredness, ill temper, and melancholy) and love him for the prince he could be; and finally, her return after being set free to try to save the beast from the murderous Gaston and villagers even though she is putting herself in harm's way.

All of these selfless and generous acts in turn ignite a spark in the beast that ultimately leads to his and everybody else's transformation; they become whole and good—resurrected in a sense—to new life. In the final ballroom dance scene of the film, Belle, the beast, the castle servants, and the villagers are gathered together as one in a restored castle, a scene that calls to mind Jesus' image of the kingdom of God as a banquet; it could serve as a vision of the resurrection. Does not the story of *Beauty and the Beast* shed new light on the story of Jesus Christ's Incarnation, Crucifixion, and Resurrection, redeeming human beings from the sin that mars their humanity and restoring them to new life? Does not the story of Jesus Christ shed light on this fairy tale?

The actor who plays Belle in the 2017 remake, Emma Watson, without any reference to Christ, captures the essence of this and even puts a name to it as she explains in an interview:

> What's so beautiful about this story as a whole is the idea that Belle is able to see past these extraneous, external, superficial qualities of the Beast. . . . I think she can see in the Beast that there's someone that's fundamentally good that has been damaged and just needs rehabilitation. He is just in need of

Continued

---

13. T. Chris Cain, "Turning the Beast into a Beauty: Toward an Evangelical Theological Aesthetics," *Presbyterion* 29, no. 1 (Spring 2003): 36.

love. . . . She is able to see deeper, and that's one of her special powers. It is her superpower: empathy.[14]

Empathy has been defined as "the capacity to understand or feel what another person is experiencing from within the other person's frame of reference, i.e., the capacity to place oneself in another's position."[15] The New Testament asserts that "God is Love" (1 John 4:8). Does not God, in becoming one with humanity in the Incarnation and embracing human ugliness in the cross, embody divine empathy, which is truly beautiful? As suggested earlier by the quotes from Dostoevsky and Augustine, is not beauty what ultimately moves human beings, makes them whole, "resurrects" them? For Christians, Jesus, as God Incarnate, the "Face of God" and the supreme expression of God in the world, embodies divine beauty.

Consider these questions as you read this book:

- How is Jesus, like Belle, treated as an outsider by the people in his society? Why are both misunderstood and treated with suspicion?

- How does Jesus show empathy and compassion? How does Jesus respond to those who are considered ugly and unlovable by his society? How does this compassion affect not only those he heals but also those around him, including his disciples, ordinary people, and religious authorities?

- What makes both Belle and Jesus truly beautiful? Is it their physical appearance or something else?

Many contemporary scholars believe the Gospels were written in the period thirty to sixty years after Jesus' death, as the generation of disciples who knew and followed him during his lifetime, witnessed the risen Jesus, and were first to proclaim his message and found Christian communities had begun to pass away.[16] The Gospels were most likely written to address particular situations and issues in the communities to which they were addressed. In this sense, the story of Jesus answered the questions or needs of a given community at a specific moment in time. The Gospel authors brought the story of the life and teachings of Jesus to bear upon their respective Christian communities.[17]

---

14. Anthony Brezican, "Beyond Beautiful," *Entertainment Weekly*, February 24/March 3, 2017, 28–29.

15. Paul S. Bellet and Michael J. Maloney, "The Importance of Empathy as an Interviewing Skill in Medicine," *JAMA* 266, no. 13 (October 2, 1991): 1831–32.

16. Johnson, *The Writings of the New Testament*, 139–40.

17. Ibid., 140.

The Gospels are all organized around two fundamental issues facing every disciple and every community of believers:

- How should one answer Jesus' question, "Who do you say that I am?"[18]
- What is demanded or required of Jesus' disciples?

The second question is examined later in this book. The first question derives directly from the community's shared faith in the Resurrection and is the central organizing question for the Synoptic Gospels.[19] When Jesus asks the disciples, "Who do people say that I am?," they give various answers: John the Baptist, Elijah, one of the great prophets of the Old Testament, a new prophet. But Jesus then turns to them and asks, "But who do you say that I am?" Peter responds, "You are the Messiah," but the Gospels clearly intend that this question be posed of every disciple, and that all answer that he is the Messiah, the Christ. But what does this mean?

The word "Messiah," from the Hebrew word *Messiach*, means "the anointed one;" the word "Christ," from the Greek word *Christos*, means the same thing. The concept of "anointed one" is closely tied to the Jewish understanding of prophets, kings, and other significant figures who were anointed with oil as a sign of their having the gift of the divine Spirit.[20] Some Jews at the time of Jesus expected a Christ or Messiah, a specially sent and anointed leader who would come and revive the ancient glory of Jerusalem and restore the Israelites to their rightful place in the political order of things. For Christian disciples living after the death and Resurrection of Jesus Christ, who had received the Holy Spirit through initiation into the Christian community, the title "Christ" carried a deeper connotation. These Christians believed Jesus had come to save not only Israel, but the whole world. Furthermore, they believed Jesus in some way embodied the presence of the God he proclaimed. The early Christians concluded Jesus was not another holy man or prophet or theologian, but was divine, from God and like God: the human face of God. They would attempt to articulate and express this belief in different ways and language in each Gospel, but all agreed on the central response to the question posed by Jesus. Below is a short synopsis of how each Gospel portrays Jesus' life, identity, and mission.

---

18. Matt. 16:13–20; Mark 8:27–29; Luke 9:18–20. In various forms this question is asked repeatedly throughout the Gospel of John. See especially John 4:29; 6:14, 68; 7:26, 40–44; 8:25; 10:24.

19. Donald L. Gelpi, *Encountering Jesus Christ: Rethinking Christological Faith and Commitment*, Marquette Studies in Theology 65 (Milwaukee: Marquette University Press, 2009), 328–37; and Raymond E. Brown, *An Introduction to New Testament Christology* (New York: Paulist Press, 1994), 74–75.

20. Christopher McMahon, *Understanding Jesus: Christology from Emmaus to Today* (Winona, MN: Anselm Academic, 2007), 96–108; Gelpi, *Encountering Jesus Christ*, 100–102.

Reflect and Discuss

In light of the description of Belle in *Beauty and the Beast* above, what are your expectations for a hero or "savior"? Are you sympathetic with those who expect a Messiah that is powerful and strong in a more traditional way? Can you see some correlation between Belle and her "superpower" and what the early Christians experienced in Jesus Christ?

Mark: The Son of God

The Gospel of Mark begins by proclaiming Jesus is the Christ, the Son of God (Mark 1:1).[21] It goes on to identify Jesus with the good news that Jesus came to preach. The question of who Jesus is serves as an organizing issue for this Gospel. Throughout Mark's Gospel, different groups of people try to figure out who Jesus is and what he is trying to accomplish. When Jesus encounters demons, they always identify him correctly, and therefore Jesus silences them.[22] In Mark's Gospel, Herod, the king of the Jewish people, wonders who Jesus is (6:13–18) and the scribes and Pharisees continually ask this question of him and one another. Jesus' question to the disciples is at the literal center of the text (8:27–30). For Mark, Jesus is the presence of the divine life and power in human history. Jesus is sent by God to heal those who are sick in body and soul. Jesus is identified as the one who has power over the seas, winds, and other forces of nature (4:35–41; 6:45–52). These powers explicitly identify him with the divine, as God alone has power over the earth and sky, over body and soul. Mark constantly portrays Jesus as having the power to subdue the forces of chaos. The author of Mark suggests that Christ's presence in the Christian community still has that power to bring about healing and peace.

Mark's Gospel opens with the preaching of John the Baptist and his baptism of Jesus (Mark 1:2–11). Before Jesus arrives on the scene, John proclaims that someone greater than himself is coming to Israel and that although John baptizes with water, the one who is coming "will baptize . . . with the holy Spirit" (v. 8). Upon being baptized by John, Jesus has a vision of the skies opening and the "Spirit, like a dove, descending upon him" (v. 10). Jesus then hears a voice proclaim from the heavens, "You are my beloved son; with you I am well pleased" (v. 11). After this the Spirit leads Jesus out into the desert for forty days where he is "tempted by Satan" (v. 13).

---

21. There is some question as to whether this phrase was present in the original text of Mark (some early manuscripts lack it), but most scholars believe it is original.

22. See Mark 1:24; 3:11; and especially 5:1–20.

This episode conveys several important elements of Mark's understanding of Jesus' identity. First, Jesus comes as a Jewish prophet, but as one who is greater than all those who have preceded him including John the Baptist. Second, the descent of the Spirit establishes his unique relationship with God, and that he is indeed the "beloved" of God. This term signifies something like a family or filial relationship with God. Third, Jesus' baptismal experience confirms John's prediction that Jesus is indeed the Spirit baptizer and therefore he has a power that comes from God alone. Finally, for Mark, Jesus' unique status does not diminish his humanness nor does it free Jesus from the trials, difficulties, and sufferings that human beings experience in this world. On the contrary, the scene ends with Jesus being led into the "desert" by the Spirit to be tempted and tested by Satan himself (vv. 12–13).

Mark's Gospel is also strongly Eucharistic. That is, the narrative foci of the story are the two accounts of the multiplication of the loaves and fishes (6:41 and 8:6) and the account of the Last Supper—the institution of what becomes known as the Eucharist in the Christian community (14:22–25). The centrality of this story makes the paschal mystery the organizing motif of the entire narrative.[23] The Eucharist represents the radical and gratuitous sharing of Jesus' own life: his earthly life, his risen life, and his Spirit. The story of the multiplication of loaves reveals Jesus as the one who offers genuine salvation—the abundance of God's providence—to all those who are willing to receive it. Eucharistic faith also affirms the power of God to raise people from the dead and it is already a participation in the glory of Christ's risen life. The Eucharist also reminds believers they are practically assimilated to Jesus if they live as he lived.[24]

Reflect and Discuss

Describe some correlations between Mark's understanding of Jesus and Belle as described in this chapter. How are their experiences similar, especially, how they are perceived by their society? What makes them different from others? How do they respond to being different in their society?

Matthew: The Living Torah

The Gospel of Matthew is less interested than Mark in the newness or uniqueness of Jesus' identity. The author of Matthew tends to view Jesus as the fulfillment of the Torah and the prophets of the Jewish faith. In Matthew, Jesus

---

23. Gelpi, *Encountering Jesus Christ*, 205–7.

24. Johnson, *The Writings of the New Testament*, 160–61.

relates to disciples and crowds primarily as a teacher and a giver of the new law. In this Gospel, Jesus gives five major discourses (teachings)[25] on the nature of the reign of God, the requirements for disciples, and the mission of Christian communities. These five discourses are reminiscent of the five books of the Torah; in a sense, in Matthew Jesus promulgates the Christian Torah and therefore acts as the new Moses. These discourses teach disciples what it means to follow Jesus. The story of Jesus' life, ministry, and destiny, particularly the paschal mystery, demonstrate the possibilities and problems of discipleship. So Jesus does not just proclaim a new Torah, but is himself a Torah, a human embodiment of the law. The author of Matthew paints a realistic portrait of what working for the kingdom practically entails: thinking, feeling, and acting with Jesus according to the plan of the Father through the power of the Spirit.

Three key parts of Matthew's Gospel demonstrate its viewpoint about who Jesus is and distinguish it from the other Gospels.

1. **The Genealogy of Jesus (Matt. 1:1–17).** This text portrays Jesus as truly human and truly Jewish by putting him in a direct line of descent from Abraham. It also connects Jesus with the story of God's saving relationship with Israel as narrated in the Old Testament. Finally, it introduces the theme of fulfillment because Jesus brings to completion and breaks the succession in a dramatic, new way. Jesus is the Messiah, a miraculous fulfillment and new beginning for the salvation history that began with Abraham.

2. **The Infancy Narrative (1:18–2:23).** This story not only introduces the primary themes of the Gospel—Jesus as the fulfilment of God's promise to Abraham—but also Jesus' birth and early life mirror the life of Israel itself. Jesus himself undergoes a journey into exile in Egypt, then back home to the Promised Land. This journey implies that Jesus himself is metaphorically the New Moses and the new Israel.

3. **Jesus' Conception by the Holy Spirit (1:22–25).** This text corrects the perceived ambiguity in Mark's Gospel about Jesus' relationship with the Spirit by insisting the Spirit relates to Jesus in a special way from the beginning. In Matthew, the baptism by John only reveals this relationship; it does not initiate it. This text also emphasizes Jesus' transcendent origins and divine Sonship by explaining Jesus' unique title in Matthew. In Matthew, Jesus is called "Emmanuel," which means "God is with us" (Matt. 1:23). This revelation will in turn come to its fulfillment in the Resurrection when Jesus promises to be with the disciples to the end (Matt. 28:20).

---

25. The five major teaching passages in the Gospel of Matthew are the Sermon on the Mount (Matt. 5–7), the Missionary Discourse (Matt. 10), the Parables of the Kingdom of God (Matt. 13), the Discourse on Living in Community (Matt. 18), and the Eschatological Discourse (Matt. 24–25). See Mark Allan Powell, *Fortress Introduction to the Gospels* (Minneapolis: Fortress, 1998), 61–84.

Sandro Botticelli's *The Annunciation* (Florence, ca. 1485-92) captures the moment in which the angel Gabriel proclaims to Mary in Nazareth that she will give birth to a son and name him Jesus (Luke 1:26–38). Though extremely confused and even frightened by this announcement, Mary accepts the word of God.

Luke–Acts: The Good News of Salvation

The author of Luke produced a two-volume narrative of the origins of Christianity: the Gospel of Luke and the Acts of the Apostles. The first volume recounts Jesus' proclamation of the kingdom, and the second volume recounts the Christian community's proclamation of the risen Christ. The first volume is about the life, message, death, and Resurrection of Jesus Christ, while the second volume is about the coming of the Spirit and its life and activity through the Christian community. Luke is remarkable because he presents an account of the origins of the Christian community that clearly links it with the historical person and work of Jesus of Nazareth.

Throughout these two volumes, Luke also invokes the theme of "fulfillment." For the author of these narratives, however, this implies not just that Jesus is the fulfillment of salvation history as it is revealed in the sacred texts of ancient Israel but also that the fulfillment of Jesus' work and mission is the Christian community, which is commissioned to bring the good news of salvation to the Gentiles and to the ends of the earth. There is a parallel between the movement of Jesus from Galilee to Jerusalem in the first volume and the movement of the proclamation from Jerusalem to Rome in the second volume. The collapse of Jerusalem (and with it many people's hopes for the future of Israel) signals the birth and expansion of the gospel throughout the world with the Resurrection and the sending of the Spirit. This theme of parallel movements appears throughout the two texts.

The innovative dimension of Luke's account of the identity of Jesus is most evident in the so-called infancy narrative (Luke 1:5–2:52), which also traces parallel movements. The infancy narrative tells the story of two births: Jesus and John the Baptist. This story sets up a prolonged theological reflection on the relationship between the two and between the two visions of God's judgment on the world that they represent. This parallelism serves two points: first, it shows how both have divinely ordained missions, and, second, it shows Jesus' superiority at every point; John is Elijah, returned to prepare Israel for the Messiah, whereas Jesus is the Messiah, the Savior and Son of God.

The infancy narrative has within it two remarkable hymns or poems that focus on Jesus and seek to interpret his birth and divine mission. These two hymns are known as the "Magnificat" (Luke 1:46–55) and the "Benedictus" (1:68–79).[26] The Magnificat, or the "Canticle (Song) of Mary," consists of Mary singing the praises of God. This song is organized around two major themes. In the first motif, Mary blesses God for what God has done for her (1:47–49). Here Mary draws a parallel between what God has done for her and God's merciful vindication of all the lowly ones who place their confidence in God. This introduces one of the primary themes of Luke's Gospel: God's special care for the lowly and dispossessed as demonstrated by Jesus' preferential care for them. Virtually every verse of the Magnificat has a parallel in the Old Testament. This in turn implies that what God is about to accomplish in Jesus fulfills every promise God has ever made to Israel.

The second major theme in the Magnificat is the juxtaposition of the power of God with those that are powerless and through whom the power of God is displayed. Through Jesus, the powerless ones, literally the "little ones" (Hebrew, *anawim*; Greek, *tapeinoi*), are exalted and favored by God. Mary herself is one such example.[27] For Luke, the God who raises the lowly, and brings down the mighty has now become present in history in the person of Mary's newborn child Jesus. Jesus, as the promised Messiah, is the one who will permanently alter the judgment of the principalities and powers of this world. This Messiah will bring a genuine peace to the world and will inaugurate the rule of justice and a time of prosperity for all people. This message of justice and concern for the poor and outcasts resonates throughout the Gospel in Jesus' words and actions. Luke places the social justice vision of Old Testament prophets and psalmists at the heart of Jesus' proclamation, ministry, and personal life.

The second hymn, the Benedictus, is sung by John the Baptist's father, Zechariah, and builds upon the Magnificat by proclaiming that Jesus comes to fulfill the covenant originally made with Abraham. This text interprets the whole covenant as a sign of divine liberation; Jesus' coming will now allow Israel to serve God in

26. Raymond E. Brown, *The Birth of the Messiah: A Commentary on the Infancy Narratives in the Gospels of Matthew and Luke*, new updated ed., Anchor Bible (New York: Doubleday, 1993), 346–55.
27. Ibid., 350–55.

holiness without fear of any enemies. Here Luke puts Jesus' messianic presence in stark contrast to the political and military vision of a number of Jewish groups at the time, whose members expected a messiah figure to liberate the Jewish people and bring peace to the world.[28] Jesus contradicts any expectations that God's peace will be established by coercion or violence. In Jesus, God comes into this world as weak, poor, and homeless, and therefore God utterly identifies with the poor. For Luke, God's power will work through this seeming weakness to transform history. Jesus is announced with traditional images of power and might, but then Luke immediately reverses these images by putting them in the context of a new-born infant lying in a feeding trough. God's power is revealed in a very unexpected and surprising way, a way that, to human beings, looks like weakness. For Luke, this ultimately implies that God's ways are not human ways, and believers must attune themselves to God's ways rather than try to force God into narrow human understandings of reality. What God has in store for the world is different from what the world expects. The best example of this in Luke's Gospel is Jesus' mother, Mary. Mary embodies the kind of disciple needed in the kingdom: she is willing to open herself totally to the power and plan of God, willing to identify with the poor and outcast, willing to accept the mystery of God's plan obediently and without testing it, and continually willing to ponder the person of Jesus Christ in her heart.

The rest of the infancy narrative develops these themes. The story claims that Jesus is conceived not by normal human means but by "the power of the Most High" (Luke 1:35). This remarkable claim immediately reveals his divine origin and mission. The rest of the Gospel employs both discourses and parables to lay out the plan of God for this world (called the reign of God). For Luke, Jesus embodies this plan. To be a follower of Jesus means accepting this plan and accepting the person of Jesus Christ. To be a follower of Jesus Christ means imitating him by thinking, seeing, and feeling as he did. It also implies working directly and practically for the reign of God that he inaugurates.

Reflect and Discuss

Belle's beauty is described as possessing various dimensions. In Luke's Gospel, which of these traits apply to Jesus? How do the Magnificat and the Benedictus portray God? Can you see similarities between Belle's and Luke's depictions of God?

---

28. Among the major religious and political factions of the Jews during this period—the Pharisees, Sadducees, Essenes, and Zealots—the latter two were the most convinced of an imminent messiah. The Essenes believed in the return of a powerful prophetic-type messiah who would usher in the final judgment of the righteous and the wicked, which would result in the end of the world. On the other hand, the Zealots expected the return of a Davidic-type warrior king to liberate Israel and reestablish an Israelite kingdom free from Roman rule. See Mark Allen Powell, *Introduction to the New Testament* (Grand Rapids: Baker Academic, 2009), 18–25.

John: The Word Made Flesh

The Gospel of John is unique in many ways. Presumably written later than the other Gospels, the author's primary theological intent is evident throughout. In John's account, Jesus' unique, divine identity serves as the organizing vision. For the author of John, Jesus' humanity reveals his divinity. Throughout his life and ministry, Jesus displays his divine identity and his awareness of his unique personal relationship with the Father and Spirit. Throughout this story, Jesus seeks to reveal and share this relationship with his followers.

John's focus and unique style of theology is evident in each of the four main sections of his Gospel. The prologue (John 1:1–18) introduces the primary themes of the Gospel, and is examined in greater detail below. The Book of Signs (John 1:19–12:50) offers an extended reflection on the mission and ministry of Jesus, his self-identity, and the nature of genuine Christian discipleship. The Book of Glory (John 13:1–20:31) reflects on the passion, death, and Resurrection of Jesus and investigates the direct implications of these events for the disciples. And lastly, the epilogue (John 21) covers the post-Resurrection period and in particular the forgiveness and commissioning of Peter. Of the numerous texts that provide rich theological reflection, the following discussion focuses on just two, texts that would shape the history of Christian theology: the prologue (John 1:1–18) and Jesus' discussion of his sending the Advocate and relationship to the Father (John 14:15–31; 16:5–33).

John's Gospel does not have an infancy narrative or a genealogy, but it does have a prologue that introduces the main themes of the Gospel and addresses the central theme of much of New Testament Christology. The prologue was probably a hymn that emerged from the Johannine community and its life of prayer and worship. It is one of the most famous and influential texts in the whole of the New Testament for the development of subsequent theology. The prologue deals directly with the identity of Jesus. The first stanza of the hymn refers to Jesus as the "Word" (*Logos* in Greek). Nowhere else in the Gospel does the author refer to Jesus as the Word. But here John, perhaps drawing on the Old Testament wisdom tradition most evident in the Psalms and the book of Proverbs,[29] refers to Jesus as the spoken word of God that creates the world "in the beginning," saves human beings through Jesus' death and Resurrection, and reveals the "glory" that is to come. It is important to remember that the term "Word" needs to be interpreted strictly in the context of the hymn of which it is an integral part. The Word was with God and is identified as God. This demonstrates that Jesus exists "in the beginning" and acts as an agent in the creation process rather than merely observing God or acting on God's behalf.

---

29. Gerald O'Collins, *Christology: A Biblical, Historical, and Systematic Study of Jesus* (Oxford: Oxford University Press, 1995), 38–44.

The hymn goes on to state that Jesus acts as the saving light of all of humanity in a battle between light and darkness that seems to encompass all reality. Jesus' personal life exhibited this struggle between dark forces and the light of God's mystery that shines through Jesus.[30] Jesus, therefore, is the revelation of the divine glory, the divine light. John declares that Jesus is the only Son of God, and that he became "flesh" and "dwelt" (*eskēnōsen*, literally "pitched his tent") with human beings. That Jesus became flesh means he took on all aspects of human life including human vulnerability, weakness, and mortality. For John, though, Jesus' human life does not obscure his deeper identity but serves as a fundamental dimension of it. Jesus' humanity reveals God's glory and makes it explicitly visible to humanity, including humanity in its most limited, fragile, and broken condition. The text goes on to state that, although no one has ever seen God, when human beings see Jesus they see the "real" face of God. The life and mission of Jesus reveals God's own intention to participate in human life, to share in the human struggle, and to deliver the truth to human beings that cannot be accessed any other way. Jesus, who is "at the Father's side" (John 1:18), unveils and represents the deep mystery that is at the heart of reality. This hymn offers a preview of the story. In the ongoing life of the church, this hymn will provide the central "Christological motif" of Christian interpretation of God and God's loving intention toward human beings.

Chapters 14 and 16 in John's Gospel fit into two wider contexts: the Book of Glory and Jesus' "Farewell Discourse" to his disciples.[31] In his Last Supper and Farewell Discourse with his disciples, Jesus expands upon the themes of his unique relationship with the Father, his love and concern for his disciples, and his desire that they should continue to share in his life through taking on his relationship with the Father and the Spirit as their own. In the first part of both chapters, Jesus tells his disciples he is going away so that he can send them an Advocate (or "Paraclete," *paraklētos* in Greek) who will defend them against the "world" (John 14:15–17; 16:7–11): the Holy Spirit. The term "Advocate" is unique to John and seems to mean something like "witness" or "defender," someone who speaks on behalf of another in a court of law.[32] The Advocate will tell them even more about God than Jesus can explain or they can understand now. The Advocate will also unite them with God and one another so they can

---

30. It is important to emphasize that the light/dark metaphor is always and only a reference to the relationship between grace and sin and must never be construed to have racial or ethnic overtones or implications. Sadly, there is a history of misinterpretation of these metaphors to infer that any kind of "darkness" is bad, less human, or unequal to those things identified as "light." For more on the history of this false interpretation and its terrible implications for racism, see James Cone, *The Cross and the Lynching Tree* (Maryknoll, NY: Orbis, 2011), and Howard Thurman, *Jesus and the Disinherited* (Boston: Beacon, 1996).

31. Brown, *Introduction to the New Testament*, 352–56.

32. See further Gelpi, *Encountering Jesus Christ*, 371.

continue Jesus' mission to the world. Jesus' Farewell Discourse brings to clarity the perspective of the author that the world faces a fundamental struggle between darkness and light. In view of this, Jesus' impending Passion and death will seem to many disciples to be the triumph of darkness over light. For John, though, the paschal mystery is essentially the fulfillment of God's plan to bring light to the whole world. The Spirit will explain this to the disciples when the time comes and will aid the disciples in the absence of Jesus himself to proclaim the good news and continue to participate, like him, in the love of the Father. As the one who sends the Advocate (John 16:7), Jesus again demonstrates his divine status as one who can give the Spirit to others.

Theologically, the central theme of John's Gospel revolves around developing insights and expanding the proclamation of the prologue concerning Jesus' unique relationship to the Father and its consequences for believers.[33] The Farewell Discourse offers one more opportunity for Jesus to express this relationship and its consequences. Jesus says, "I have told you this in figures of speech. The hour is coming when I will no longer speak to you in figures but I will tell you clearly about the Father" (16:25). Jesus goes on to explain how he came from the Father and will now return to the Father (16:28). He then turns to the disciples and asks them whether they believe this to be true (16:30–31). Not unlike the scenes in all the Gospels where Jesus asks the disciples, "Who do you say that I am?" here Jesus is also asking his disciples if they understand clearly his identity and if they have faith in him. The faith they have in him and his message should be the same as they have in God. Jesus assures them that if they have this faith they will have the power to continue his mission and their joy "will be complete" (16:24). In all this, Jesus lays out explicitly, in a way that will guide all future Christian theology, the interrelationship between the Father, Jesus the Son, and the Spirit. John's Gospel dramatizes the intimate connection between Jesus Christ and the Christian understanding of God as Trinity.

Reflect and Discuss

The Gospels tell a story of the triumph of love over injustice, hate, and violence. How does the fairy tale of *Beauty and Beast* shed new light on the story of Jesus? What stands out as central to both stories? In what ways are they similar? Where do they differ? Does the character of Belle help you to better understand the character of Jesus as he is presented in the Gospels?

---

33. Ibid., 362.

The Epistles of Paul

This section will focus exclusively on the epistles, or letters, of Paul, not because the other letters have no implicit or explicit theology of the identity of Jesus Christ, but because Paul holds a special place among the New Testament authors. Paul asserts he personally saw the risen Christ—probably the only New Testament writer to have done so. In this encounter, Jesus commissioned him to preach the good news to the whole world (Gal. 1:11–12, 16). Although Paul never meets or has any interactions with the earthly Jesus and makes few allusions or references to his personal life or message in the way that the Gospels do, he does directly experience the risen Christ. So, for Paul, there is never any question as to Jesus' real identity: because Jesus died he must be a real human being like everyone else; but because of Paul's extraordinary experience, in which, he says, "God . . . was pleased to reveal his Son to me" (Gal. 1:15–16), Paul understands Jesus as something other than an ordinary human being. Paul argues that the Resurrection revealed God is working in and through Jesus in a unique and powerful way. The paschal mystery (the Passion, death, and Resurrection of Jesus Christ), therefore, reveals something new about human beings and about the mystery of God. In this sense, the paschal mystery is the central focus of all of Paul's letters.

Paul reflects in considerable detail on the theological significance of Jesus' Resurrection in light of his own experience and in light of the experience of others that was directly communicated to him. That is, Paul developed his theological account in light of the needs and questions of the Christian communities to which he wrote. Paul's theological vision therefore emerged situationally and pastorally rather than narratively as is the case in the Gospels. He consistently interprets the risen Christ as a continually present reality that affects every dimension of human life. The events of Jesus' death and Resurrection always simultaneously reveal something about the meaning and significance of human lives and serve as a guide for how people should interpret reality and react to events.

It is possible to tease out two (always interconnected) themes that run throughout the Pauline Epistles. One strand expresses, as in the Gospels, Jesus' identity and unique relationship to the Father and the Spirit and his unique fulfillment of the divine plan revealed to Israel. The other strand considers how Jesus's life, death, and Resurrection reveal something about God's plan for human beings and even for all creation. These two strands together determine the identity and mission of Jesus for Paul.

Like the Gospel writers, Paul is Jewish and therefore often looks to the Jewish Scriptures for images and references to help him explain the reality of Jesus. Paul also realizes he must make sense of Jesus Christ for those Gentiles in the Christian community who have little or no understanding of Jewish Scriptures or traditions. For this reason, Paul often draws on hymns or prayers that were known and probably regularly sung or recited by the Christian communities to which he writes.[34] These hymns, probably tied to celebrations for baptism and the Eucharist, reflect the shared faith of the Christian communities, whether the members come from Jewish or Gentile backgrounds. By drawing on these hymns, Paul is helping these communities deepen their understanding of Jesus Christ and the saving plan of God that he reveals. Below are four fundamental images or motifs that run throughout Paul's letters and offer basic insight into Paul's understanding of Jesus Christ and his meaning for humanity.

The Christological Hymn of Philippians 2:6–11

Who, though he was in the form of God,
did not regard equality with God something to be grasped.
Rather, he emptied himself,
taking the form of a slave,
coming in human likeness;
and found human in appearance,
he humbled himself,
becoming obedient to death,
even death on a cross.
Because of this, God greatly exalted him
and bestowed on him the name
that is above every name,
that at the name of Jesus
every knee should bend,
of those in heaven and on earth and under the earth,
and every tongue confess that
Jesus Christ is Lord,
to the glory of God the Father.

Jesus Christ as the New Adam

Paul often refers to Jesus as the new Adam (see particularly 1 Cor. 15:22; Rom. 5:12–20). Paul is referring here to the first human in the Old Testament creation accounts, in which God fashions a clay doll and then breathes life into it, creating the first human being (Gen. 2:4–7). The second Adam, Jesus, breathes new life

---

34. New Testament hymns include the "Lukan Canticles" (Luke 1:46–55, 67–79; 2:13–14, 28–32) and several "Pauline" hymns (Phil. 2:6–11; Col. 1:15–20; Eph. 1:3–14; 5:14; 1 Tim. 3:16; 2 Tim. 2:11–13). The earliest Christians would have used these hymns in worship, along with a few standard prayers such as the Lord's Prayer (Matt. 6:8–13; Luke 11:2–4). These hymns come from a variety of Jewish and early Christian sources and probably were already familiar to the first readers of the New Testament texts. See Brown, *Introduction to the New Testament*, 232–33, 286–89, 489–91.

into humanity, offering it salvation from sin and death. Here Paul is contrasting two types of life: on the one hand, the normal physical and psychological life of human beings, which is often confounded by sin and chaos and ultimately ends in death; and on the other, the fullness of life filled by the Holy Spirit that overcomes the chaos of sin and promises the resurrection from the dead for all who believe.[35] As Paul states: "For just as in Adam all die, so too in Christ shall all be brought to life" (1 Cor. 15:22). Furthermore, Paul and the early Christian communities that personally experienced the Resurrection of Christ and this dramatic outpouring of the Spirit were transformed by it and found in it an abundant and overflowing new source of life and hope (Rom. 5:17, 20). They also were commissioned by the risen Christ to share this experience through preaching and the new form of shared communal life that Paul referred to as the church.

Jesus, as the new or final Adam, also has universal overtones in that the salvation offered by God in Jesus is not just for one religion, race, or generation of people, but is for the whole human race. In this sense, Jesus inaugurates a new era in human history and creates fundamentally new conditions under which all people can live their lives. The designation of Jesus as the new Adam not only implies that Jesus existed in God from the beginning, as mentioned in the Gospels (discussed in more detail below), it also confirms that Jesus as a human being overcomes death and thereby uniquely reveals God's plan to save all people from death. Paul, like the Gospel writers referring to Jesus as the new David and the new Moses, views Jesus as fulfilling the promises God made to the Jewish people. For Paul, Jesus Christ comes to breathe new life into the whole of humanity and all of creation.

Jesus Christ as the Kenōsis of God

In one of the earliest and most famous hymns in all of Paul's letters (Phil. 2:6–11),[36] Paul declares that Jesus, "though he was in the form of God" did not consider that his equality with God was something he needed to hold on to; "rather, he emptied himself" and "humbled himself" to become a human being and, even more, a "slave." The Greek term for "emptying" used here (*kenōsis*) implies that Jesus represents the literal outpouring of Godself into a human, physical, and historical existence with the goal of raising humans back up to a divine level with God.[37] In Jesus, God's generosity becomes a kind of self-forgetfulness that

---

35. Gelpi, *Encountering Jesus Christ*, 122–23.

36. See the sidebar for the full text of this hymn.

37. The image of the *kenōsis* or "self-emptying" of Jesus through his Crucifixion signals an early theological interpretation of the paschal mystery concerning the person and work of Jesus Christ. This Christological theme has been used consistently throughout the history of the church as a recognition of God as being present with those who suffer and against their oppressors; see, for example, Gustavo Gutierrez, *A Theology of Liberation: History, Politics, and Salvation*, rev. ed. (Maryknoll, NY: Orbis, 1988), 299–302. See David Noel Power, *Love without Calculation: A Reflection on Divine*

allows God to enter the sheer vulnerability and fragility of human life and experience even the depths of human weakness and suffering. The hymn goes on to say that, because of this self-emptying, God the Father has made a human name—Jesus—a divine name to which "every knee should bend" and "every tongue confess that Jesus Christ is Lord."

The transformation of the human name into a divine name conveys what is accomplished by the life of Jesus and especially the paschal mystery. Because Jesus is the New Adam—truly human—his transformation implies that all humanity and even creation itself is raised up and exalted in and through him. God's self-emptying affects not just the self-identity of Jesus but the identity and destiny of all humanity. For Paul, one cannot separate the divine/human identity of Jesus from the saving significance this reality represents for humanity in general. By entering so completely into human experience, God transforms it as well, giving it a new meaning and purpose.

Reflect and Discuss

Paul's understanding of Christ and his "power" to save human beings has significant connections with Belle and her power in *Beauty and the Beast*. Consider the relationship between Paul's Christology and beauty. What connections do you see? How is Christ different from Belle? What more does Christ have? How does their beauty affect others?

Jesus Christ as the Image of the Invisible God (Col.1:15–20)

The first stanza of the hymn in Paul's Letter to the Colossians proclaims that Jesus Christ is "the image of the invisible God" (Col. 1:15).[38] The hymn goes on to state that "all things were created through him and for him" (v. 16). Here

---

Kenosis: "He Emptied Himself, Taking the Form of a Slave," Philippians 2:7 (New York: Crossroad, 2005), 63–118; Gerald F. Hawthorne, "The Imitation of Christ: Discipleship in Philippians," in *Patterns of Discipleship in the New Testament*, ed. Richard N. Longenecker, McMaster New Testament Studies (Grand Rapids: Eerdmans, 1996), 163–80. For a historical analysis of the theme of *kenōsis* see Walter Kasper, *The God of Jesus Christ* (New York: Crossroad, 1984), esp. 189–97.

38. There is a large scholarly debate concerning the composition, authorship, and dating of the Letter to the Colossians. The letter is undoubtedly Pauline in its overall message and style, meaning it follows closely enough to the rhetorical and theological style of Paul's other writings to be viewed at least as having come from one of his disciples, possibly Timothy or a later leader closely connected to the Pauline school. Brown, among other scholars, considers Colossians a "pseudonymous" work, meaning it was likely penned by someone other than Paul though borrowing his name and speaking from the authority of Paul. More recently, other scholars, such as Luke Timothy Johnson, have argued for a more direct influence between Paul and the Letter to the Colossians later

is one of the earliest declarations of the preexistence of Jesus (a theme that is echoed in the opening hymn of the Gospel of John) and that Jesus shared in the act of creation with God. The hymn goes on to explain why this knowledge is important for human beings: Jesus comes "to reconcile" the world to God (v. 20). In other words, God's divine presence in the human person of Jesus not only reveals God's saving intentions toward humanity, but accomplishes this reunion. This reiterates the ongoing theme in Paul that the way Jesus is related to God has implications not only for Jesus' identity but for all human beings as well. The hymn proclaims that God not only desires to dwell with human beings, but that God desires that human beings participate in God's own life as well—another theme echoed in the prologue to John's Gospel.

Jesus Christ and the Spirit

Paul consistently identifies the risen Christ as the one who both gives the Spirit to disciples and in turn is given to believers by the Spirit.[39] The complete interrelationship and mutual giving of the risen Christ and the Spirit finds echoes in the Gospels and completes their accounts. Paul, however, offers an even more startling claim. On two occasions Paul identifies the risen Christ directly with the Spirit. In the aforementioned passage discussing Jesus as the last Adam, Paul concludes with the claim, "The first man, Adam, became a living being, the last Adam a life-giving Spirit" (1 Cor. 15:45). Here Paul seems to be claiming a functional relationship or identity between Jesus and the Spirit in that both give life to humanity. In other words, Jesus has the fullness of the Spirit and mediates or gives it to human beings in a way that transforms and enlivens them analogous to how the "first Adam" mediated physical and psychic life to the rest of humanity.

On another occasion, Paul states that "the Lord is the Spirit" (2 Cor. 3:17–18). Paul often uses the term "the Lord" to refer to the risen Christ, although on this occasion he is using it to refer to his Spirit. In this context, Paul is comparing the story of Moses in the book of Exodus (34:29–35)—and the covenant that he represents—with the new reality brought about through Jesus Christ. Moses witnessed the glory of God and his face shone in a way that prevented the Israelites from looking directly at him. But that glory eventually faded away. Paul goes on to claim that the glory revealed by Jesus in the Resurrection will

---

in his life, likely during his imprisonment. According to this view, Paul would have been involved in the message and teaching of the letter even if a scribe physically wrote the letter. In either case, as Mark Allan Powell helpfully argues, the theology, or specifically, the Christology presented in this letter conforms to Paul's understanding of Jesus Christ found throughout his letters. See Brown, *Introduction to the New Testament*, 610–17; Johnson, *The Writings of the New Testament*, 347–58; and Powell, *Introducing the New Testament*, 360–63.

39. See further, James D. G. Dunn, *The Christ and the Spirit*, vol. 1, *Christology* (Grand Rapids: Eerdmans, 1998), 113–67, and Johnson, *The Writings of the New Testament*, 103–5.

not fade away, but will in fact grow and develop continually in the hearts of believers until the day that they share directly in the glory of God. As Paul states, "All of us, gazing with unveiled face on the glory of the Lord, are being transformed . . . from glory to glory" (2 Cor. 3:18).

The identification of Jesus here with the Spirit signifies that the Resurrection reveals the true and complete fullness of Jesus' life. Jesus is and always has been part of the life of God, and this vital shared life is fully revealed in the practical cooperation of Jesus and the Sprit in enabling the saving plan of God. Jesus and the Spirit together not only reveal something radically new about God, but convey this reality by transforming all those who believe; believers are caught up and transformed by this revelation. For Paul, after the Resurrection, the work of the Spirit and the work of Jesus coincide in directing humanity on the same path as Jesus: from life and death to resurrection and glorified life with God. For Paul, Jesus' identity and its effects on human beings always intersect.

CHRIST-FIGURES IN FILM

Reel to Real

Greg Zuschlag

Despite their iconic power, Christ-figures are not limited only to characters projected on the big screen or those who fill the pages of fictional narratives but also can be found in real life. In this century, exemplary Christ-figures include Mohandas K. Gandhi, Martin Luther King Jr., Dorothy Day, Ceasar Chavez, Mother Theresa, and Oscar Romero and other martyrs of the El Salvador civil war.

But a Christ-figure does not have to be an individual person; communities of people can and often do represent Christ as well. One example of communities functioning as Christ-figures might be the L'Arche movement founded in 1964 by Canadian Catholic philosopher, theologian, and humanitarian, Jean Vanier (1928–).[40] L'Arche (French for "the Ark") began when Vanier and Father Thomas Philippe invited two men with intellectual disabilities to live in community with them. In 2018, there were 147

Continued

40. See *https://www.larche.org/en_US*; *https://www.larcheusa.org/*; *http://www.jean-vanier.org/en /home*. For a good, short autobiographical treatment of Vanier, see Michael W. Higgins, "Messy Love: Jean Vanier's l'Arche," *Commonweal* 136, no. 9 (2009): 10–14, *http://digitalcommons.sacredheart.edu /cgi/viewcontent.cgi?article=1031&context=mission_pub*. The movement includes 165 ecumenical and interfaith, faith-based communities in thirty-seven countries around the world (eighteen in the United States).

CHRIST-FIGURES IN FILM: REEL TO REAL *Continued*

L'Arche communities in thirty-five countries, supporting about five thousand adults with disabilities.[41] Two types of people form these communities: those with special cognitive disabilities, called "core members," and "those who come to share life with them" in community and accompany them in the "activities of daily life: creating home and supporting core members in sharing their gifts within the house and the larger community." These people, called "assistants," dedicate themselves to building "relationships of mutual care and support with persons with disabilities."[42]

What makes L 'Arche a compelling communal Christ-figure? Do not Vanier and his "disciples," the assistants, act like Christ in their care, compassion, and the sacrifice of their "normal" life for those "core members" with whom they live? Do not the "able-bodied" assistants "save" the disabled people who suffer from their physical and cognitive limitations and who have often been rejected, alienated, and abused because of their physical condition by the larger society? According to Vanier and his fellow assistants, such an understanding of the direction of "salvation" is reversed, or in a more complex manner, the community itself as constituted by those with special disabilities and those with "ordinary" disabilities—like the majority of us "wounded" yet highly functional persons—create something like the biblical covenants of old and the covenant remade in Jesus Christ: this is what makes a Christ-like salvation truly manifest. A fundamental principle underlying the model and mission of L'Arche's Charter states, "Weakness and vulnerability in a person, far from being an obstacle to union with God, can foster it. It is often through weakness, recognized and accepted, that the liberating love of God is revealed."[43] This belief, which obviously applies to the core members, when seen with the eyes of Christ, actually applies more to those of us whom society sees as superior, strong, and invulnerable; virtual superheroes in the eyes of all and especially those who are considered (and consequently often consider themselves) weak, needy, and worthless.

Theologian John Swinton describes L'Arche as practicing a form of Christology: "Here we see clearly that the weak become strong and that the foolishness of this world turns out to be the glory of God. In Jesus,

Continued

---

41. See the L'Arche USA website for more information: *https://www.larcheusa.org/who-we-are /larche-international-2/.*

42. *Https://www.larcheusa.org/participate/become-an-assistant/.*

43. L'Arche Charter, *http://www.larche.ca/en/members/vision_future/larche_charter/.*

CHRIST-FIGURES IN FILM: REEL TO REAL Continued

Vanier sees a paradigm of strength in weakness." Swinton quotes Vanier: "Jesus is the starving, the parched, the prisoner, the stranger, the naked, the sick, the dying. Jesus is the oppressed, the poor. To live with Jesus is to live with the poor. To live with the poor is to live with Jesus." Swinton concludes, "In the weakness and vulnerability of the profoundly intellectually disabled Vanier discovers Jesus. If such lives are truly fully human, then 'being human' can no longer be understood in terms of power, strength, intellect and ability. To be with the intellectually disabled is to realize what it means to be human." As Vanier says, "Growth begins when we begin to accept our own weakness."[44]

Such observations open the way to understand L'Arche communities as prototypical Christ-figures in much the same way that Belle is presented in this book's discussion. Vanier describes the work of L'Arche as a deeply personal and relational form of imitating Christ. Vanier acknowledges how difficult it is for the majority of us to be "constantly close to people who are weak and in pain, whose limits and handicaps are irremediable, and to be with them as friends." We resist acknowledging our own "limits, vulnerability, and weakness, the places of violence, of fear and of anguish." Vanier suggests, "Many in our societies reject people with disabilities, unable to see the person and his or her value underneath the handicap."[45] Vanier sees L'Arche as a "place of friendship and of a communion of hearts, where we live in covenant relationships together. It is not just about things *for* people with disabilities, but to be with them, to create a home with them. . . . We transform them but they also transform us."[46]

Vanier's reflections on the L'Arche communities convey the Christian perspective on what constitutes genuine holiness and Christian discipleship. For Christians, the goal of human life is to embody Christ in today's broken yet healable world, making the Incarnation, the Word made flesh, continually present in the here and now, opening the way for all persons to meet the living Christ and be transformed ("saved") by him in new, unexpected, and refreshing ways.

Having read this chapter, consider the following questions:

Continued

44. John Swinton, "A Embodied Theology," Jean Vanier: Transforming Hearts, *http://www.jean-vanier.org/en/his_message/a_theology/a_embodied_theology*.

45. Jean Vanier, "Towards a Transformational Reading of Scripture," *Comment Magazine* 30, no. 2 (Fall 2012): 60.

46. Ibid.

CHRIST-FIGURES IN FILM: REEL TO REAL Continued

- How does Jesus change or even reverse our ordinary understanding of power, strength, intellect, and ability? Why does Jesus seem to be drawn so much to the weak and vulnerable? What does this tell us about his fundamental mission and message? How is Jesus transformed by his interaction with weak and vulnerable people in this society? How are they transformed by him?

- For the New Testament authors, why does Jesus' proclamation of the good news lead to his arrest and execution? What does this say about Jesus' mission and his humanity? What does it say about God if Jesus is truly in a unique relationship with God?

For Further Exploration

Identify other reel (fictional) and real (nonfictional) Christ-figures. One place to start is the Wikipedia entry on fictional Christ-figures: https://en.wikipedia.org/wiki/Christ_figure. Note, however, that this entry contains a warning: "This section may contain indiscriminate, excessive, or irrelevant examples." How would you use this chapter to develop criteria for discerning who counts as an authentic Christ-figure as opposed to a "false" or Antichrist-figure?[47]

For further exploration, consider what criteria are most important in identifying Christ-figures. Try to identify additional individual and communal Christ-figures. Some often overlooked figures worth considering are

- Jaime Escalante, a real person who is the basis for the protagonist of the film, *Stand and Deliver* (1988)

- Susan Burton, coauthor of the autobiography *Becoming Ms. Burton: From Prison to Recovery to Leading the Fight for Incarcerated Women*[48]

- Roy Batty and police officer K in *Blade Runner* (1992) and *Blade Runner 2049* (2017)

---

47. See the sidebar on Superman in chapter 2 of this book for discussion of the myth of redemptive violence. See also Russell Dalton, "(Un)making Violence through Media Literacy and Theological Reflection: Manichaeism, Redemptive Violence, and Hollywood Films," *Religious Education* 110, no. 4 (July–September 2015): 395–408 and Anton Karl Kozlovic, "The Structural Characteristics of the Cinematic Christ-Figure," *Journal of Religion and Popular Culture* (2005), *https://web.archive.org/web/20050223221011/http://www.usask.ca/relst/jrpc/art8-cinematicchrist.html*.

48. Susan Burton and Cari Lynn, *Becoming Ms. Burton: From Prison to Recovery to Leading the Fight for Incarcerated Women* (New York: New Press, 2017).

Review Questions

1. What is the meaning of the term *Christology?*
2. What is the paschal mystery and what is its significance for Christology?
3. For whom was the New Testament written?
4. List some of the major themes and images from the Old Testament that the New Testament authors use to interpret Jesus.
5. What are the Gospels and how are they unique in the New Testament?
6. What is the fundamental question at the heart of each Gospel?
7. How do each of the Gospel writers answer that fundamental question?
8. What is unique about Paul's perspective on Jesus Christ?
9. For Paul, what is the relationship between Jesus and Adam?
10. What is *kenōsis* and how does it relate to Paul's understanding of Jesus?
11. How does Paul identify the relationship between Jesus and the Spirit?

Discussion Questions

1. For the authors of the New Testament, why is it important that Jesus was a fully human person?
2. Why are there four different Gospels rather than one story of the life of Jesus, and what do we learn from their unique perspectives?
3. Given that Jesus came to preach "good news," why, according to the Gospels, was Jesus publicly executed? How does Paul understand the significance of Jesus' death?
4. Compare and contrast the prologue of the Gospel of John with Paul's notion of *kenōsis*.
5. Would Jesus' life still have the same meaning without the Resurrection? Why or why not?

Additional Resources

PRINT

Brown, Raymond E. *The Birth of the Messiah: A Commentary on the Infancy Narratives in the Gospels of Matthew and Luke.* New updated ed. Anchor Bible. New York: Doubleday, 1993.

————. *An Introduction to New Testament Christology.* New York: Paulist, 1994.

Dungan, David L. *A History of the Synoptic Problem: The Canon, the Text, the Composition, and the Interpretation of the Gospels.* 1st ed. Anchor Bible. New York: Doubleday, 1999.

Gelpi, Donald L. *Encountering Jesus Christ: Rethinking Christological Faith and Commitment.* Marquette Studies in Theology, no. 65. Milwaukee: Marquette University Press, 2009.

Gutierrez, Gustavo. *A Theology of Liberation: History, Politics, and Salvation.* Rev. ed. Maryknoll, NY: Orbis, 1988.

Hellwig, Monika, *Jesus the Compassion of God.* Wilmington, DE: Michael Glazier, 1983.

Johnson, Elizabeth A. *Consider Jesus: Waves of Renewal in Christology.* New York: Crossroad, 1990.

Johnson, Luke Timothy. *Living Jesus: Learning the Heart of the Gospel.* Reprint ed. San Francisco: HarperOne, 2000.

———. *The Writings of the New Testament.* 3rd ed. Minneapolis: Fortress, 2010.

Longenecker, Richard N., ed. *Patterns of Discipleship in the New Testament.* McMaster New Testament Studies. Grand Rapids: Eerdmans, 1996.

McMahon, Christopher. *Understanding Jesus: Christology from Emmaus to Today.* Rev. ed. Winona, MN: Anselm Academic, 2013.

Powell, Mark Allan. *Fortress Introduction to the Gospels.* Minneapolis: Fortress, 1998.

Power, David Noel. *Love without Calculation: A Reflection on Divine Kenosis: "He Emptied Himself, Taking the Form of a Slave," Philippians 2:7.* New York: Crossroad, 2005.

Reid, Barbara, *Taking up the Cross: New Testament Interpretation through Latina and Feminist Eyes.* Rev. ed. Minneapolis: Fortress, 2007.

Schussler Fiorenza, Elizabeth. *In Memory of Her: A Feminist Theological Reconstruction of Christian Origins.* New York: Crossroad, 1983.

———. *Jesus: Miriam's Child, Sophia's Prophet; Critical Issues in Feminist Christology.* 2nd ed. London: T&T Clark, 2015.

Wright, N. T. *Christian Origins and the Question of God.* 1st North American ed. Minneapolis: Fortress, 1992.

———. *The Challenge of Jesus: Rediscovering Who Jesus Was and Is.* Downer's Grove, IL: IVP Books, 2015.

OTHER MEDIA

The Early Christians: The Incredible Odyssey of Early Christianity. DVD video. 2 discs. San Francisco: Ignatius, 2011.

The Face: Jesus in Art. DVD video. Written by James Clifton. [United States]: WNET, distributed by PBS, 2001.

2

CHAPTER

Jesus Christ: Ancient to Contemporary Perspectives

The documents in the New Testament were written for real people in response to the questions, trials, and struggles they faced every day.[1] The authors of these documents saw in Jesus Christ, and particularly in his suffering, death, and Resurrection, the answer to their problems, needs, and hopes. They saw in Jesus Christ the embodiment of his own proclamation that God is love and is present with all human beings in their daily, ordinary lives. These authors are called "evangelists," as explained in the last chapter, precisely because they proclaim the "good news" of Jesus Christ and the difference that he makes for every human life.[2]

The evangelists tried to make sense of Jesus Christ within the religious context of late Second Temple Judaism and the cultural context of Hellenism.[3] These writers also wanted to connect this understanding of Jesus with the life of the Christian community they experienced. Later generations of Christians collected, revised, organized, and preserved these documents, confident that all people needed to hear the "good news" of Jesus Christ. They believed Jesus' life and message would respond to the deepest needs and hopes of the human heart no matter the times or context.

---

1. For a good introduction to the New Testament, see Luke Timothy Johnson, *The Writings of the New Testament*, 3rd ed. (Minneapolis: Fortress, 2010); Mark Allan Powell, *The Gospels* (Minneapolis: Fortress, 1998); Corrine L. Carvalho, ed., *Anselm Companion to the New Testament* (Winona, MN: Anselm Academic), 2014.

2. Recall from the last chapter that the Greek word *euangelion* means "good news," so "evangelists" are those that proclaim the good news of Jesus Christ.

3. For an overview of the period of time referred to as Second Temple Judaism, see Corrine L. Carvalho, *Encountering Ancient Voices: A Guide to Reading the Old Testament* (Winona, MN: Anselm Academic, 2006), 338–71.

The Gospel authors used narrative to make a statement about Jesus' identity; in effect, they answered the question, "Who is Jesus?" They related the story and identity of Jesus and the meaning of his death and Resurrection to their audiences. Later generations of Christians would need to draw on other theological methodologies and strategies to respond to their own unique intellectual and cultural contexts. But the fundamental questions would remain basically the same: Who is Jesus Christ for people living here and now? Why does he make a difference for this people in this time and place? What should ordinary people do in the light of his life, mission, and message? The good news that Jesus is the "image of the invisible God" (Col. 1:15) who desires to make "his dwelling among us" (literally "pitch his tent among us"; John 1:14) and live with us and die for us remains the heart of the Christian revelation and the central Mystery that Christian theology would address in the ensuing two thousand years in every cultural and social context that it encounters. These continue to be the fundamental questions and basic tasks of theology at this moment of human history as well.

Hellenism

As Christianity grew and spread throughout the Roman Empire at the dawn of the second century, one of the significant challenges Christians faced was to explain and "make sense" of their beliefs to a culture with no connection to or familiarity with the Jewish world out of which Christianity emerged. The cultural foundation of the Roman Empire was Hellenism.[4] *Hellenism* refers to the language and cultural heritage of the Greek Empire and its enduring systems of thought, politics, education, social organization, religion, and artistic expression. Central to this way of thinking was Plato's hypothesis that all of reality is divided into two fundamental parts: (1) the unchanging, invisible, spiritual realm of ideas, and (2) the physical and material realm of individual things, inevitable change, and illusion. Over time, Plato's hypothesis developed into an entire system of thought: there exists a fundamental split (a dualism) between spirit and matter; ideas or forms and physical things; souls and bodies. As stated above, this overarching dualism created a way of viewing the world and human experience as fundamentally divided between the real and eternal realm of ideas, and the illusory and deceptive, unreal world of time and physical existence. This dualistic worldview formed a critical challenge to Christians trying to explain the fundamental proclamation of their faith: that God became a human being and dwelt in time and space in the created world.

---

4. For more on Hellenism, see Jaroslav Pelikan, *Christianity and Classical Culture: The Metamorphosis of Natural Theology in the Christian Encounter with Hellenism* (New Haven: Yale University Press, 1993), and Richard Tarnas, *The Passion of the Western Mind: Understanding the Ideas That Have Shaped Our World View* (New York: Ballantine, 1991), 98–138.

Christian leaders and theologians interpreting the New Testament in terms of the logic of Hellenism faced many of the same challenges that their contemporaries faced in trying to explain the revelation of God's identity as three-in-one.[5] Given the extreme dualism of Hellenistic Roman culture, it seemed almost impossible to believe that God—the absolute, unchanging, and utterly timeless One—would even care about the world "below," let alone be born as a human being, as a child with parents in a remote and strange culture, have a real life, and be executed as a criminal. There seemed to be no way to make sense of these assertions. Furthermore, even for those willing to accept that God had somehow become "incarnate"[6] (i.e., that God had taken on flesh and dwelt with human beings), there remained the complex problem of how to interpret the relationship between the divine and human elements of Jesus' identity. These two issues—how God became human and the relationship of humanity to divinity in the person of Jesus of Nazareth—dominated Christological discussions and debates for the rest of the Greco-Roman period.

Reflect and Discuss

Consider as you continue reading this chapter how Belle saves the beast. How does her love and empathy change not just the beast, but the whole situation of the palace, her people, and their village? To what aspects of Belle does the term *beauty* really refer and how does it "save" people? How are we like the beast? How are we like the people in the palace that have been turned into objects? How are we like the people in the village where Belle comes from?

How Can God Become Human?

Initially, most attempts at explaining the Incarnation fell into two logical, but ultimately problematic, patterns.[7] One was characterized by a tendency to

---

5. See John J. Markey, *Who Is God? Catholic Perspectives through the Ages* (Winona, MN: Anselm Academic, 2016), 25–46.

6. The term *Incarnation* as referring to the simultaneous existence of the human and divine in Jesus was first used in the second century. Its first definition and common usage is attributed to Melito of Sardis (d. 180). See Johannes Quasten, *Patrology*, vol. 1, *The Beginnings of Patristic Literature* (Westminster, MD: Newman, 1952), 242–45; Karl Rahner, ed., *Encyclopedia of Theology: The Concise 'Sacrmentum Mundi'* (New York: Seabury, 1975), 690–99; and Gerald O'Collins, *Christology: A Biblical, Historical, and Systematic Study of Jesus* (Oxford: Oxford University Press, 1995), 164–75.

7. See further Johannes Quasten, *Patrology*, 1:268–72. For a good summary of the controversies and debates of this period, see John Courtney Murray, *The Problem of God: Yesterday and Today* (New Haven: Yale University Press, 1964), 31–78; see also Jaroslav Pelikan, *The Christian Tradition:*

presume that God only "inhabited" or "seemed" to have a body, but that Jesus Christ was not literally a human person like other people. This approach was termed *Docetism*, from *dokein*, Greek for "to seem."[8] At the other end of the spectrum was the hypothesis that Jesus Christ was a real human being, but not literally the God who is the source of all things. Those who asserted this explanation usually believed either that Jesus was "adopted" by God to participate in some unique way in God's sovereign life (known as *adoptionism*), or that Jesus was actually some kind of lesser deity specifically created by God to act as an intermediary between God and human beings (known as *subordinationism*). Subordinationists actually maintained that Jesus was divine in some way, but, as a created being, he was not fully divine in the same way as the one God who created everything. Nevertheless, Christian Scripture insisted that Jesus was a real human being and who was simultaneously divine and continually participating in a single divine life with the Father and the Spirit. These two attempts to resolve the tension between Jesus' humanity and divinity appeared reasonable to an extent, but the church as a whole eventually judged them to be incorrect. The problem of articulating an understanding of Jesus that avoided these two mistakes became the dominant task of Christian theology for the next three hundred years.[9]

The solution to this question emerged most fully with the beginning of a series of church "councils" or gatherings (called the Ecumenical Councils, meaning universal or worldwide gatherings of bishops and other church leaders) that began with the Council of Nicea in the year 325.[10] Eventually, these meetings created a single, agreed-upon formula that would serve as the standard statement of Jesus' simultaneously divine and human identity. This formula, commonly referred to as the Nicene Creed, made clear that neither the Son nor the Spirit were "created." Rather, both exist in a unity of existence with the Father; all together they comprise what Christians mean by the term *God*. For Christians, God is a common unity of life—one being, made up of the relationship between the Father, Son, and Spirit (generally referred to as the *Trinity*).[11] The creed also affirms the complete humanity of Jesus. The creed states that the Lord

---

A History of the Development of Doctrine, vol. 1, *The Emergence of the Catholic Tradition (100–600)* (Chicago: University of Chicago Press, 1975). J. N. D. Kelly, *Early Christian Doctrines*, rev. ed. (San Francisco: HarperOne, 1978), 138–63, 280–344. See also John P. Galvin, "Jesus Christ," in *Systematic Theology: Roman Catholic Perspectives*, ed. Francis Schussler Fiorenza and John P. Galvin, 2nd ed. (Minneapolis: Fortress, 2011), 264–67.

8. The various religious-philosophical schools of thought that are collectively known as *Gnosticism* generally embraced Docetism.

9. See Richard Tarnas, "Dualistic Christianity," in *Passion of the Western Mind: Understanding the Ideas That Have Shaped Our World View* (New York: Ballantine, 1993), 130–37.

10. See further Colman J. Barry, ed., *Readings in Church History* (Westminister, MD: Christian Classics, 1985), 81–105; O'Collins, *Christology*, 177–97; and Markey, *Who Is God?*, 40–42.

11. For a more thorough explanation of the Christian understanding of God as Trinity, see Markey, *Who Is God?*

Jesus Christ "came down from heaven" and was born to a woman named Mary. This implies that he had a real life: he grew from a child into an adult, he had emotions, feelings, and experiences that shaped and formed him, he felt desire, pain, frustration, sadness, joy, and boredom. Like all human beings, he eventually died. The creed goes on to affirm what makes his experience unique in human history: he rose from the dead, ascended to his original place with the Father, with him shared the Spirit with all humanity, and will come again in "glory" to act as judge of human history.

The Nicene Creed and other subsequent church councils insisted that genuine (or "orthodox") theology must maintain that Jesus was fully human and fully divine. The question of how this was possible, however, would continue to provoke discussion and debate for another two hundred years.[12]

CHRIST-FIGURES IN FILM

Superman and the Myth of Redemptive Violence
Greg Zuschlag

"He'll be a god to them"—Superman's father, Jor-El

Superman is often identified as a Christ-figure. A wealth of insightful observations and analyses about Superman as a Christ-figure exists both in print and on the internet, especially in reference to the Superman movies: the original *Superman: The Movie* and *Superman II* (1978, 1980, directed by Richard Donner) and the *Man of Steel* "re-boot" (2013, directed by Zach Synder). One of the screenwriters from the 1978 film confessed that he borrowed Christian themes and symbolism in Christopher Reeves's portrayal of Superman.[13] Anton K. Kozlovic, who has written more articles on Christ-figures in film than any other scholar, identifies "twenty Superman-Jesus parallels" plus eight Christlike personality "traits" in his article, "Superman as Christ-Figure: The American Pop Culture Movie Messiah."[14]

Continued

---

12. See Luke Timothy Johnson, *The Creed: What Christians Believe and Why It Matters* (New York: Doubleday, 2003); and Gerald O'Collins, *The Tripersonal God: Understanding and Interpreting the Trinity* (New York: Paulist Press, 1999), 114–27. For a very good chart laying out the first four Ecumenical Councils and their relationships to one another, see Christopher McMahon, *Understanding Jesus: Christology from Emmaus to Today* (Winona, MN: Anselm Academic, 2013), 147.

13. See Daniel Dickholtz, "Steel Dreams: Interview with Tom Mankiewicz," *Starlog* (December 16, 1998): 67–71.

14. Anton K. Kozlovic, "Superman as Christ-Figure: The American Pop Culture Movie Messiah," *Journal of Religion & Film* 6, no. 1, *http://digitalcommons.unomaha.edu/jrf/vol6/iss1/5*.

CHRIST-FIGURES IN FILM: SUPERMAN AND THE MYTH *Continued*

While earlier films are comparatively subtle in presenting Superman as a Christ-figure, Synder's 2013 retelling, especially in Warner Brothers's marketing of the film, makes the portrayal explicit.[15] CNN and the *Hollywood Reporter* produced pieces on how the director harnessed Christ-like parallels in his version of the Superman myth, and how the studio's marketing department created a whole internet-social media campaign to promote the film to Christian ministers and congregations.[16] Moreover, Warner Brothers enlisted Craig Detweiler, a professor at Pepperdine University, to write a document of sermon notes for ministers entitled "Jesus—the Original Superhero" for a website aimed at religious leaders.[17] Finally, a website devoted to Christian youth ministry provides one of the best examples of how some view the film positively through a Christological lens.[18]

Mark Sandlin, a Presbyterian minister, rejects Superman as a Christ-figure because Superman resorts to violence to combat violence and

Continued

---

15. Literally "Over-man" in German, which can also be translated as "Superman." The term was popularized in Friedrich Nietzsche's 1883 philosophical work, *Thus Spoke Zarathustra*.

16. Jennifer Vineyard, "'Superman: Man of Steel' Director Zack Snyder on Superman's Christ-Like Parallels," CNN Entertainment, June 16, 2013, *http://www.cnn.com/2013/06/14/showbiz/zack-snyder-man-of-steel*, and Pamela McClintock, "The Superman Gospel, According to Warner Bros.," *Hollywood Reporter*, June 18, 2018, *http://www.hollywoodreporter.com/news/superman-gospel-warner-bros-570668*.

17. Though the original website, *manofsteelresources.com*, has subsequently been taken down, at the time of this printing Craig Detweiler's treatment, "Man of Steel Sermon Notes: 'Jesus—The Original Superhero,'" was available at *https://www.dropbox.com/s/0oedjbj2k8op0ko/Man-of-Steel_Sermon-Notes_Final4.pdf*.

18. Phil Trotter, "Senior Youth: Man of Steel Mirrors Jesus," Resourced! Tried and True Resources for Anglican Youth Ministries in NZ, *https://www.anglicanyouth.org.nz/resources/studies/senior-youth-studies/man-of-steel-mirrors-jesus*.

CHRIST-FIGURES IN FILM: SUPERMAN AND THE MYTH Continued

upholds "might-makes-right solutions," a common narrative in Hollywood cinema.[19] In his post he references the "myth of redemptive violence," a concept developed by the theologian and peace activist Walter Wink (1935–2012). For Wink, "the myth of redemptive violence is the story of the victory of order over chaos by means of violence. It is the ideology of conquest, the original religion of the status quo. . . . The prize goes to the strong. Peace through war, security through strength: these are the core convictions that arise from this ancient historical religion, and they form the solid bedrock on which the Domination System is founded in every society."[20]

Wink suggests that comic book superheroes incarnate perfectly the myth of redemptive violence. Superman "intervenes in the lives of people he encounters without ever challenging them to evaluate their beliefs and values or expose themselves to the anguish of transformation. He merely manipulates the environment. Villains are relegated to the outer darkness but not redeemed from their bondage to evil or restored to true humanity."[21]

How does Superman as a Christ-figure compare to Belle? Superman appears to be a human but is actually an alien, whereas Belle is what she appears to be: an attractive yet independent-minded young woman. Superman intervenes to save the planet from destruction without really empowering humanity to cooperate, whereas Belle practices patience, learns to accept the beast's limitations, and ultimately saves the beast through her "superpower" of empathy and compassion.

Questions to Consider: Superman versus Belle

• For many people, Superman is a more obvious Christ-figure than Belle. Why might this be so?

Continued

---

19. Mark Sandlin, "Superman vs. Jesus," *Huffpost*, June 14, 2013, *https://www.huffingtonpost.com/mark-sandlin/superman-vs-jesus_b_3444361.html*. A particularly problematic dimension of *Man of Steel* is that Superman kills General Zod instead of re-imprisoning him in the Phantom Zone. This "broke what comic book fans traditionally call 'the rule' of the superhero ethos: Thou shalt not kill, even though you can. The very point of Superman, in particular, was that he always found a solution without killing, which would have been so easy for him to do." See Trotter, "Senior Youth: Man of Steel Mirrors Jesus."

20. Walter Wink, *The Powers That Be: Theology for a New Millennium* (New York: Doubleday, 1998), 48.

21. Walter Wink, *Engaging the Powers: Discernment and Resistance in a World of Domination* (Minneapolis: Fortress, 1992), 19.

CHRIST-FIGURES IN FILM: SUPERMAN AND THE MYTH *Continued*

- Which Christ-figure, Belle or Superman, exhibits more similarities to the traditional Christian understanding of Jesus? Explain?
- Identify similarities and differences in how Belle and Superman save humanity. Which is the more Christlike savior? Why?

How Can the Divine and Human Coexist in One Person?

After Nicea, Christian theologians struggled to explain and make sense of the relationship between Jesus' humanity and divinity as asserted in the Nicene Creed. The ordinary, rational explanations of this relationship tended to fall between two poles. On the one hand, some theologians held there was only one identity or nature in Jesus, which implied that the divine overwhelmed the human dimension in Jesus; this was called *Monophysite*—meaning "one nature"—Christology. On the other hand, some argued there were two distinct natures in Jesus and when these were combined they created a "third" or hybrid reality that made Jesus truly human, but utterly different from any other kind of human; this was termed *Apollinarism*, after a major proponent of this position. One group of theologians, known as the Alexandrian school, continually struggled against the Monophysites and Apollinarians to maintain the integrity of the two natures in Christ but nevertheless often seemed to diminish the real humanness of Jesus in favor of his divinity. Another group of theologians, generally referred to as the Antiochene school, insisted on the completeness of Jesus' humanity (i.e., a humanity that included a body and a soul), and found themselves at odds even with the Alexandrians in their attempt to remain faithful to the scriptural insistence on the humanity of Jesus.[22] At stake was the need to assert clearly the "unity-in-distinction" of the divine and human natures in Jesus, while at the same time formulating a description of human nature (called *anthropology*) that adequately expressed the unity of Jesus' soul and body in a way that made the Incarnation a genuinely historical event. Developing an adequate anthropology (i.e., an understanding of human nature in general) became a fundamental Christological problem in the West for centuries to come.[23]

---

22. For an in-depth analysis of these developments, see Lewis Ayres, *Nicaea and Its Legacy: An Approach to Fourth Century Trinitarian Theology* (Oxford: Oxford University Press, 1984), 167–272; O'Collins, *Christology*, 184–201; and Galvin, "Jesus Christ," 266–74. For a very accessible chart displaying these positions, see McMahon, *Understanding Jesus*, 135–36.

23. See Donald L. Gelpi, *Encountering Jesus Christ: Rethinking Christological Faith and Commitment* (Milwaukee: Marquette University Press, 2009), 417–79; Jaroslav Pelikan, *Jesus through the Ages: His Place in the History of Culture* (New Haven: Yale University Press, 1985), 71–82.

Two great leaders of the fifth-century church, Cyril[24] and Nestorius,[25] attempted to bring to clarity the problem between asserting *that* there is a union of the divine and human in Jesus and explaining *how* that union comes about. Nestorius, however, demonstrated a tendency to diminish the humanity of Jesus because of his reliance on systematic Platonic accounts of this union. Cyril, on the other hand, insisted on the essential unity of the natures in Jesus even if this seemed to defy standard Platonic logic. These controversies eventually lead to the Council of Chalcedon in the year 451. The church leaders and theologians there reached an agreement that became known as the Chalcedonian Formula: there exist two natures in one person in Jesus Christ. This means that Jesus is a single living, historical reality with two distinct and unmixed natures. This formula—two natures in one person—then became the norm for all subsequent Christological reflection in most Christian churches. This formula basically settles these complex Christological debates and helps to make sense of one of the central New Testament claims about God: that God became a human being in Jesus Christ (in the Incarnation).

Furthermore, the Chalcedonian Formula attempts to explain why these debates were important in the first place. Namely, that the Incarnation is an act of God's love that "saves" human beings by enabling them to participate in the divine life in a new and dramatic way. Because Jesus becomes a real human being, human beings, in turn, can participate in God's life. This formula brings to clarity the claim of the Cappadocian[26] theologian Gregory of Nazianzus that any aspect of humanity not taken on (or "assumed") by Jesus cannot be saved by the action of God's love in the Incarnation.[27] Because of Jesus' Resurrection, Christians are convinced that all human beings will experience life again in the future. This implies however, that for any part of human nature to be redeemed by Jesus Christ it must be fully taken on by the Second Person of the Trinity. If the divine, however, only occupies a human body but does not have a mind or soul, there is no assurance that an individual's mind or soul will be redeemed. But if Jesus is truly a human being, then Christians can genuinely hope that the whole of their identity will be "raised" and allowed to participate in the divine life in the resurrection of the dead that awaits all creation. The whole human person (body and soul, mind and matter) has been united with God in Jesus Christ and will be reunited with the divine life on the last day.[28]

---

24. Kelly, *Early Christian Doctrines*, 317–23.

25. Ibid., 310–17.

26. See Markey, *Who Is God?*, 43.

27. Gregory of Nazianzus, *Ep.* 101. See also Gregory of Nyssa, *Anti-Appolinarian Writings*, Fathers of the Church 131 (Washington, DC: Catholic University of America, 2015), 91–120.

28. For an excellent analysis of how the Incarnation saves humanity in this perspective, see Gelpi, *Encountering Jesus Christ*, 490–98.

Theotokos and the Nestorian Controversy

Nestorius, the Bishop of Constanti-
nople from 428 to 431 and a member
of the Antiochene school of Christology, taught that Jesus' human identity and divine identity were distinctly
separate realities. The historical person of Jesus, therefore, must be distinct from the eternal reality of the
Son of God. Only in the Incarnation
did the two natures come together.
Thus he rejected the practice, common in his day, of referring to Mary
as the *Theotokos*, the "Mother of
God" (literally "God bearer"). For
Nestorius and his followers, Mary
was the mother of Jesus Christ (as
a human being) and not literally the
Mother of God, the Second Person
of the Trinity; thus he argued that her
title is more properly "Christ-bearer"

The "Theotokos" icon of Mary as
the God-bearer led to a theological
debate that ultimately resulted in the
Nestorian Schism over the correct
interpretation of the Incarnation and
the two natures of Jesus Christ.

(*Christotokos* in Greek).[29] Nestorius's teachings were deemed heretical at
the Council of Ephesus (431 CE) and again at the Council of Chalcedon
in 451 CE.[30] These councils resulted in the Nestorian Schism; a few Asian
and Middle Eastern churches continue to embrace Nestorian Christology.

After Chalcedon: Why Does God Become Human?

Anselm of Canterbury[31]

The first great theologian of the Middle Ages, Anselm of Canterbury (1033–
1109), wrote a book entitled *Why a God-Man?* (*Cur Deus Homo*). Anselm,

---

29. See further Nestorius, *Second Letter of Nestorius to Celestine of Rome*, http://www.tertullian.org
/fathers/nestorius_two_letters_01.htm.

30. Norman Tanner, *Decrees of the Ecumenical Councils*, 2 vols. (Washington, DC: Georgetown
University Press, 1990), 1:37–104.

31. See Brian Davies, et al., *Anselm of Canterbury: The Major Works* (Oxford: Oxford University
Press, 1998), and Anselm of Canterbury, *Why God Became Man*, trans. Joseph M. Colleran (Albany,
NY: Magi Books, 1969).

instead of delving into the details of whether or how God became human, sought to explain in a fundamentally new cultural context why human redemption required an Incarnation and particularly the death and Resurrection of Jesus (the paschal mystery). Anselm began by assuming that the Nicene Creed and the Chalcedonian Formula are true and proceeded to expand upon their meaning for the people of his time. This marked a new phase in Christology as theologians began to move past the controversies of the Hellenistic period and to focus more on analyzing and clarifying the formulas they had received, explaining how this received tradition applied to the spiritual needs of a new generation of Christians.[32]

Anselm developed his understanding of Jesus Christ in the light of a very different culture than that of the New Testament and the Roman Empire. Anselm was writing in a time when most people lived in rural communities— farms or small towns that depended for their survival on the fact that all the inhabitants could live and work together with some level of mutual trust and respect. Disagreements, marital infidelities, broken promises, and crimes like theft and violence could tear a small community apart. This kind of instability could endanger people's lives. Furthermore, Northern Europe had just come out of hundreds of years of political chaos, violence, and lawlessness. The most important aspect of life in Anselm's world therefore was justice. Justice in this culture meant restoring the balance in the family, community, or society that had been lost by breaking a rule or committing a crime. This notion of restoring balance and "making things right" shaped all dimensions of early medieval society.

Anselm developed his Christology with the hypothesis that human sinfulness had caused such a great imbalance in the world that without somehow restoring the original created order all humanity would necessarily and justifiably be damned. For Anselm, divine justice required a full repayment before the balance could be restored. Repayment demands a "perfect proportionality" between the good denied God through sin and the good offered to God in repayment for sin. From this point of view, justice requires that God punish sin before forgiving it. In other words, God's justice demands that humans be stripped of the goods acquired through sinful actions before God can fully restore the imbalance their sin has created. So, for Anselm, God's justice requires that God actively and aggressively punish sinful creatures. "Satisfaction" for sin cannot be achieved by punishment for sin, but only after punishment can some kind of repayment or restoration be achieved. But how is this possible, given the enormity of the imbalance and the inadequacy of human beings to give to or do anything meaningful for God?

The solution to this seemingly insoluble dilemma for Anselm is a God-Man. Only God can satisfy God, although humans should be the responsible for their own debt. So only a God-Man (the Incarnation) can restore perfect proportionality and achieve the balance humans lost through sin. Anselm

---

32. See O'Collins, *Christology*, 197–201, and Galvin, "Jesus Christ," 276–77.

asserts the Incarnation is a rational and necessary satisfaction for human sin-fulness. Furthermore, Jesus' death—an inevitable consequence of perfect obedi-ence to God in such a sinful world—could fulfill the conditions of satisfaction required by divine justice. Because Jesus' death was worthy not of punishment but reward, Jesus offered this reward to humanity as a means of restoring the goods lost through Adam's sin and all subsequent sins. Jesus Christ, the divine/human person, merited salvation but did not need it for himself; consequently, Christ was able to give this salvation to the rest of humanity. This means that the great imbalance is corrected and perfect proportionality is not only restored but enhanced: humanity wins back the eternal life it had lost through sin, as well as a new source of overflowing merit it could not otherwise have attained.

Anselm's Christology marks the beginning of a long tradition of interpret-ing the Incarnation in terms of how it is relevant to the salvation of humanity rather than simply how it is possible.[33] Nevertheless, Anselm's interpretation does have its limitations in that his understanding of atonement as the satis-faction of divine justice tends to contradict the biblical and patristic witness by claiming that God needs the suffering and death of an innocent man to substi-tute for the penalty of sin to which each person is liable. While this explanation responds to a cultural mode of thinking in his time, it tends to cast God as vin-dictive, punitive, and dependent on the requirements of an external justice that forces God to demand "satisfaction."[34]

Reflect and Discuss

Compare Belle and Superman. Which is closer to the God-Man Anselm is describing? What is the difference between their "superpowers"? Why is it so important that Jesus is fully human for Anselm? What is the signifi-cance of Belle's humanity for her story?

Peter Lombard[35]

Peter Lombard (1100–1160) wrote a book called *The Sentences*, which would become the basis of all medieval theology. Lombard developed *The Sentences* along similar lines as Anselm but tended to explain the concept of satisfaction

---

33. For further history and analysis of atonement theories, see Gelpi, *Encountering Jesus Christ*, 482–90.

34. For a detailed analysis of the significance of Anselm's theory, see Walter Kasper, *Jesus the Christ* (New York: Paulist Press, 1974), 219–21, and Galvin, "Jesus Christ," 274–78.

35. See Jason L. A. West, "Aquinas on Peter Lombard and the Metaphysical Status of Christ's Human Nature," *Gregorianum* 88, no. 3 (2007): 557–86.

as primarily changing human beings, by freeing them from deadly pride and empowering them to love again. Atonement for Lombard restores to humans the hope of eternal salvation and the remission of eternal punishment owed because of sin. Atonement, however, does not necessarily imply a vindictive understanding of punishment, nor does it require an innocent death for satisfaction. Although Peter left the details of his interpretation somewhat vague, he emphasized the restoration of humanity over the reparation of the injury done to God. He focused more on the "merits" won by Christ for humanity and the conviction that only a divine/human could actually restore humanity to its original balance with God and God's plan for creation.[36]

Thomas Aquinas

In the great medieval synthesis of theology, the *Summa Theologiae*, Thomas Aquinas (1225–1274) advanced beyond the foundational work of *The Sentences* in the number and depth of Christological questions addressed. By assimilating the work of the Greek philosopher Aristotle[37] and his critique of Plato, Thomas revolutionized medieval Christological thinking in two important ways: (1) by offering a fuller philosophical account of the human person (anthropology); and (2) by articulating a more plausible account of how the world works in general (cosmology).[38] This new perspective enabled Thomas to more accurately reflect on the New Testament witness about the humanity of Jesus and the ways in which Jesus saves humanity. By moving beyond the overly dualistic philosophy of the Hellenistic period, Thomas was able to give a more realistic account of the life and personality of Jesus Christ. He was also able to provide a new explanation of the meaning of the Incarnation for the people of his culture.[39]

For Thomas, the Incarnation is a part of the larger "cosmological" framework of God's offer of love to human beings and all creation (this offer of love is called *grace*). Thomas envisions the Incarnation as the culmination and revelation of the many "incarnations" (God becoming present in various ways to people) that characterize a world permeated by grace at all levels. For Thomas life is a journey or a project in which every human person must engage. Jesus Christ

36. See Donald L. Gelpi, *The Firstborn of Many: A Christology for Converting Christians* (Milwaukee: Marquette University Press, 2001), 3:369–71.

37. See Markey, *Who Is God?*, 64–67.

38. *Summa Theologiae*, part 3, available online at *http://www.newadvent.org/summa/4.htm*. Questions 1–26 focus on the philosophical and theological foundations of Christology and questions 27–59 focus on the life of Jesus.

39. See Brian Davies, *Aquinas* (New York: Continuum, 202), 140–49; O'Collins, *Christology*, 202–10; Kent Emery Jr. and Joseph P. Wawrykow, eds., *Christ among the Medieval Dominicans: Representations of Christ in Text and Images of the Order of Preachers* (Notre Dame, IN: University of Notre Dame Press, 1998), 7–25, 175–237.

comes as the leader and guide of a new or renewed humanity heading into a new future. This future is characterized as life with the freedom and the power to live as God intended human beings to live. Thomas moves Christology away from a static system of broken and restored dualistic order to a Spirit-driven journey of a people and the working out in history of the divine plan. In the *Summa*, Thomas explains how Jesus reveals this divine plan, explains and demonstrates its practical consequences through his life and actions, and then gives his life for it in the paschal mystery. Jesus is literally the way, the truth, and the life for Thomas Aquinas.[40]

Reflect and Discuss

Consider the description of Jean Vanier and the L'Arche community described in chapter 1. Do their lives give you a sense of the "practical consequences" of the paschal mystery? How do they manifest Thomas's vision of life as a dynamic project of trying to make Christ present both in our lives and in the social conditions of the world in which we live? Consider the ways in which the L'Arche community represents Christ not only to its members but to all those who come into contact with it. How does the L'Arche community symbolize the Spirit-driven journey of people working out the divine plan in history?

Although there was no absolute rational necessity for God to become human, Thomas saw a relative necessity in that it allowed God to reveal Godself fully to humanity and evoke the fullest response of love in return. The Incarnation shows people how to truly live, to undo the effects of sin, and to offer everyone a share in the divine life as adopted children. Thomas insists that the personal union of the divine and human in Christ is unlike any kind of known natural union. Nevertheless, although this union was unique in human history, it could be known and comprehended to some extent.

Aquinas explains this union by an adaptation of Aristotelian metaphysics.[41] This allowed him, through complex reasoning, to affirm the Chalcedonian Formula in a new and intriguing way. Thomas described Jesus as a human instrument of the Word (Logos), but an instrument of a very special kind, in that he was a free individual agent of divine action. So the Word remains divine, but also allows Jesus to be its unique agent or active presence

---

40. John 14:6. See further Thomas F. O'Meara, *Thomas Aquinas: Theologian* (Notre Dame, IN: University of Notre Dame Press, 1997), 108–51.

41. Markey, *Who Is God?*, 64–67.

in human history. As one commentator states, "The result is that the events in Jesus' life are sacramental; in this or that biblical event, striking or ordinary, the divine is extended through the man Jesus. There is no miracle which is purely divine, no touching gesture which is only human."[42] So Thomas supplies a novel account of the Incarnation whereby the two natures operate in a unified way in the one person of Jesus while still remaining distinct. In other words, two kinds of human acts flow from Christ, which can be distinguished but never fully separated. Although there were many problems, questions, and discrepancies in Thomas's account of the Incarnation, it would nevertheless lay the foundation for much future discussion and debate about the meaning of the Incarnation.

Duns Scotus

The English Franciscan theologian Duns Scotus (1266–1308) was one of those who, although accepting much of Thomas's basic premise about the validity of the Incarnation, disputed his specific formulation of the relation of the divine and human in Jesus and disagreed with him over the meaning of this unique identity of the person of Jesus.[43] Scotus worried that Thomas had reduced Jesus to being a mere "agent" of the Word, and did not give his human nature its own proper vitality and meaning. This in turn led him to a different interpretation of the meaning and motivation of God becoming human.

Scotus examined the notion of "person" and found, like Thomas, earlier Hellenistic accounts of it to be too individualistic and dualistic. Scotus viewed persons as primarily relational entities and social beings. Scotus reasoned that individual human beings receive their existence from other humans and they find the fullness of their identity through social relations exemplified by love. Scotus therefore concluded, like Aquinas, that persons are fundamentally relational, but also that there is some dimension of the person which is "incommunicable," meaning totally unique to that person. So, for Scotus, a human person is both relational and incommunicable. These two dimensions define the unique singularity of each person and give a person full human autonomy. Scotus believed that Jesus' unique identity was not merely acting on behalf of the Word,

---

42. O'Meara, *Thomas Aquinas: Theologian*, 134. Sacraments are signs, symbols, or events (including rituals and stories) that enable humans to encounter or experience God's presence in the world and in their lives in a unique and distinct way. For a further explanation of sacraments, see Rahner, *Encyclopedia of Theology*, 1477–78, and John J. Markey, *Creating Communion: The Theology of the Church* (Hyde Park, NY: New City, 2004), 147–65.

43. See Alexander Broadie, "Duns Scotus and William Ockham," in *The Medieval Theologians: An Introduction to Theology in the Medieval Period*, ed. G. R. Evans, 1st ed. (London: Wiley-Blackwell, 2001), 250–68; Mary Beth Ingram, *The Philosophical Vision of John Duns Scotus: An Introduction* (Washington, DC: Catholic University of America Press, 2004), 1–21; Richard Cross, *Duns Scotus on God* (London: Routledge, 2016); Kasper, *Jesus the Christ*, 242–43.

The creche, or nativity scene, became a central element of Franciscan medieval spirituality, as it highlighted the humanity of Christ as a fragile infant. It was used as a way of teaching the inherent value and worth of humanity as created in the image of God just as the Son of God was born as a real human infant.

but that his human identity could only be understood in terms of his relationship to the divine communion of love called God. Jesus, therefore, was precisely human as the Incarnation of the Word. This incommunicable reality served as the essential truth of Jesus' personal identity. As such, Jesus' unique personhood could only be understood through the interaction of his two natures; they could not really be understood separately. Although he is not really disagreeing with Thomas—as he is clarifying his analysis—the conclusion he draws is very different from that of Aquinas.

Scotus insists Jesus' unique identity as divine and human implies God must have decided to become human before creation, not as a consequence of sin, but as a part of the divine plan from the beginning. This means the Second Person of the Trinity would have become human even if Adam had not sinned and humanity had not "fallen." God created the world so that God could become part of it. God desired not only to love all things, but that all things might love God in a perfect way. The fact that sin had entered the world meant Christ came as its redeemer in a way that would not have happened if humanity was not lost to sin. This puts Christ at the center of God's creative intent: the whole universe is created for the sake of Christ. Scotus believes the world was created out of love and for the full manifestation of the divine love in human history and human lives. The Incarnation, therefore, is the one absolutely true thing humans can know about God and about God's plan for creation. That "merits" overflow from his life and particularly his death is not accidental, but further reveals the extent of God's love for humanity.[44]

Martin Luther

Martin Luther (1483–1546), writing more than two hundred years after Thomas Aquinas and Duns Scotus, held a less optimistic view of history, religious and political institutions, and human nature. Luther lived in a time a great instability and social change. He thought about Jesus and how he saves people in personal and individual terms. Though Luther never wrote a systematic treatise on Christology, he, like earlier medieval theologians, accepted the Nicene Creed and the Chalcedonian Formula as settled doctrine and instead investigated what these beliefs meant for people of his culture. For Luther, the primary question was not how does a God-man save humanity in general, but rather how does the divine-human person of Jesus Christ effect, change, and save *me*? Luther sought to understand how Jesus personally and directly saves individuals from the chaos and sinfulness of their own lives by offering them hope for salvation beyond life in this world. Luther devoted much of his mature life to intense reflection upon the meaning of Jesus Christ for ordinary people and upon the meaning of his life for their salvation from a world of corruption, instability, and sin.[45]

In his career as an Augustinian priest and scripture scholar, Luther had been heavily influenced by his study of Saint Paul and the early Christian theologians. He tended to accept the traditional view that Jesus was the messianic mediator foretold by the prophets who brought about the reconciliation of opposites: God and humans, the divine and creation. Luther's innovation was to move the symbol of the cross to a central position in his theology. For Luther, the cross serves as the focal point and entry into understanding the utter mystery of God. The cross confronts human beings with the horrifying knowledge of the extent of human sinfulness and the realization of how thoroughly lost they would be without God becoming a human being.

Luther takes his understanding of human "original" sin and its consequences directly from Saint Augustine. Augustine taught that human nature is utterly depraved through the disobedience of Adam and Eve in the Garden of Eden (Gen. 3). Augustine named this act of disobedience and God's banishing of human beings from paradise the "Fall." Because of the Fall there is nothing human beings can do to advance their own salvation. Jesus, though, was

---

44. See Pelikan, *Jesus through the Ages*, 122–32.

45. See Oswald Bayer, "Martin Luther (1483–1546)," in *The Reformation Theologians: An Introduction to Theology in the Early Modern Period*, ed. Carter Lindberg (Oxford: Blackwell, 2002), 51–66; Dietmar Lage, *Martin Luther's Christology and Ethics*, Texts and Studies in Religion 45 (Lewiston, NY: Mellen, 1990); Marc Lienhard, *Luther: Witness to Jesus Christ; Stages and Themes of the Reformer's Christology* (Minneapolis: Augsburg, 1982); Tarnas, *Passion of the Western Mind*, 232–47.

absolutely obedient to the Father, even to death on the cross. Jesus offers people a way out of their predicament. If a person believes in Jesus Christ, God's mercy and love will be revealed to them. They discover they cannot earn or attain this love by any work or merit of their own, but that it exists through the free action of God in Jesus symbolized most clearly in the Crucifixion. Jesus, as a divine-human person, reconciles God and humanity by the cross and restores for humanity the possibility of participating in God's love, a participation they had lost through the Fall.

Luther asserted the absolute mystery and hiddenness of God, such that God can only be known through God's own self-revelation. The Incarnation, and particularly the cross, reveals God to humanity. What it reveals, though, is the difference between God and human beings. It demonstrates the "otherness" of God and the complete freedom of God to be or act however God chooses. For Luther, in the Incarnation Jesus did not cease in any way to be God: God freely chose to be human so as to come into the world as one who serves. It is God who dies for humanity, and it is God who restores the relationship between God and humans that was lost through sin. God's power and freedom is revealed through the Incarnation, because it is always God who takes the initiative in the relationship with creation. God reconciles humanity to Godself precisely through becoming a divine-human person. For Luther, without Jesus there could be no relationship between God and humans, only a vast abyss of anger and enmity.

Luther's Christology understood salvation in increasingly dramatic terms: the Incarnation was a drama of the relationship between the Father and the Son, which signified, or dramatized, the relationship between God and humanity. Given his extreme pessimism on the fallen state of human nature (rooted in the thought of Augustine and Anselm), this drama had to end in violence and death. By satisfying the Father's violent rage against humanity, however, Jesus' Resurrection means the final act will be a dramatic demonstration of the Father's love and mercy. Humans can only know about this drama and its effects through revelation, because the deeper reality of God ultimately remains hidden and mysterious, only known through actions of the Son and Spirit in the Incarnation.

Reflect and Discuss

How does Belle represent Luther's understanding of the power of Christ to save us? Do you see a connection to the way that Belle and the power of beauty restore the broken, ugly world that the ugly prince and the world surrounding him have fallen into because of his earlier behavior?

John Calvin: Jesus as Prophet, Priest, and King

John Calvin, a Swiss Protestant Reformer, interpreted the significance of Jesus in terms of how his life, death, and Resurrection achieved human salvation. That is, for Calvin, like Luther, the primary question was, "How does Jesus save us?" Calvin answered this question by expanding upon the threefold office of Jesus as prophet, priest, and king, an understanding that dates to Eusebius (ca. 260–340). In the role of prophet, Calvin saw in Jesus the perfect teacher of the Law given by God to Moses in the Old Testament as well as the perfect fulfillment of the Law as the very Word of God himself. In the role of priest, Calvin understood Jesus as the perfect and only intermediary between the wrath of God and the sinfulness of humanity. In Jesus' death and Resurrection, Calvin understood Jesus as both the priest who intercedes on behalf of the people and simultaneously the sacrifice to God. And in the role of king, Calvin understood Jesus, through the Resurrection, to be the only true leader and source of authority for the church.

Neglecting Chalcedon: From the Enlightenment to Modernity

The Quest for the Historical Jesus[46]

The Enlightenment,[47] that period in European history between the later sixteenth and the end of the eighteenth centuries characterized by the revolutionary ascendency of science, human reason, and individual autonomy, basically abandoned the notion of the Incarnation and viewed Jesus in completely "natural" terms. The Enlightenment viewed Jesus as a truly remarkable person, one of the most important and innovative teachers in human history. Jesus was often considered to be a great philosopher who developed a rich new synthesis of morality, social ethics, and personal spirituality.[48] For these thinkers, this synthesis actually constituted a new type of religion based on love and natural morality. But for most of the intellectual leaders during the Enlightenment, there was no sense

---

46. See C. H. Talbert, ed., *Reimarus: Fragments* (Philadelphia: Fortress Press, 1970); Friedrich Strauss, *The Life of Jesus Critically Examined*, trans. George Eliot (Philadelphia: Fortress Press, 1972); William Wrede, *The Messianic Secret* (Cambridge, UK: Clark, 1971); and Albert Schweitzer, *The Quest for the Historical Study: A Critical Study of Its Progress from Reimarus to Wrede*, trans. James M. Robinson (London: Black, 1911).

47. See Tarnas, *Passion of the Western Mind*, 248–323; Markey, *Who Is God?*, 70–73.

48. See Pelikan, *Jesus through the Ages*, 168–81.

in which one could call Jesus God. In fact, Enlightenment scholars generally agreed that the "divinity" of Jesus was something ascribed to him by his followers to indicate their own beliefs and the high esteem in which they held him.

This view of Jesus as a moral teacher and spiritual philosopher dominated much of Western thought into the modern period. At the beginning of the modern period (roughly from the nineteenth century until the mid-twentieth century), Jesus was seen by many scientific and intellectual leaders as an important historical person hidden behind layers of religious myth and theological interpretation in the New Testament and in the centuries following. This view led to the emergence of a movement known as the "search for the historical Jesus," which sought to discover the "real" historical Jesus behind this complex tradition of interpretation. Taking place after the French Revolution, and in light of its historical significance, these writers saw in Jesus a social activist who came to preach against organized religion and the oppressive and outdated traditions of his society. These scholars made a fundamental distinction between the message of social and political revolution that Jesus preached and the cult of personality that Jesus' disciples developed after his death. Furthermore, they argued, Jesus' disciples misconstrued and "spiritualized" Jesus' radical message and instead created a new form of organized religion that worshipped Jesus instead of following his message.[49]

Using a razor and glue, Thomas Jefferson cut out all of the words and phrases that referred to Jesus' divinity, miracles, or the supernatural and instead created a Bible that simply told the story of Jesus as a great teacher and an example of truly moral living.

49. See O'Collins, *Christology*, 212–22.

For thinkers steeped in the scientific mind-set of the Enlightenment, the key was to focus on the "Jesus of history" rather than the "Christ of faith." In other words, Jesus of Nazareth was a real human being who brought a specific life and message; Jesus Christ was merely a myth or symbol of the union of God and humanity that may have meaning to some people but does not reflect Jesus' opinion about himself, nor is the myth historically verifiable. Any parts of the New Testament that speak of Jesus as divine or supernatural are "mere" theology and should be disregarded in the search for the real Jesus of Nazareth. This led to a great number of nineteenth-century "lives of Jesus," biographies of Jesus that portrayed him as everything from the kind of social activist listed above to a philosopher and itinerant teacher.

The Second Stage in the Quest for the Historical Jesus[50]

In 1906, this project was called into question by Albert Schweitzer in his book *The Quest of the Historical Jesus*. Albert Schweitzer would later become one of the most prominent men of the twentieth century, because of his work as a composer, medical doctor, physicist, and Nobel Peace Prize recipient. Schweitzer analyzed a great number of these nineteenth-century lives of Jesus and discovered they often tended to reflect the personal and professional interests of their authors. In other words, social activists portrayed Jesus as a social activist, philosophers painted him as a philosopher, and so on. Schweitzer believed Jesus belonged to a now extinct social, cultural, and religious context that could not adequately be translated into contemporary life. He believed, therefore, that the attempt to discover the historical, human Jesus was unattainable. Schweitzer not only considered the search for the authentic Jesus of history to be useless but also believed all the theological developments that emerged after Jesus' life to be irrelevant and to constitute a religious belief system that was not sustainable in the scientific era.

In the early part of the twentieth century, other predominantly Protestant scripture scholars and theologians inverted the quest of the nineteenth century and claimed that it was precisely the "Christ of faith" that serves as the primary object of the New Testament and remains as the most important revelation for contemporary life. For these scholars, it was not really important to identify Jesus' actual historical data or his personal self-understanding. Rather, his passion, death, and Resurrection count as the defining event for the Christian tradition. These thinkers presumed that whatever and whoever Jesus was before this dramatic event, he was transformed by the Resurrection. His followers in

---

50. See N. T. Wright, *The Challenge of Jesus: Rediscovering Who Jesus Was and Is* (Downer's Grove, IL: IVP, 2015), 13–33.

turn, were faithfully recording their experience of this transformed Jesus Christ and the mission that he entrusted to them in the New Testament. Because these scholars rejected the possibility or necessity of the historical recovery of the life of Jesus of Nazareth, they also tended to reject the need to explain, validate, or translate the meaning of the Chalcedonian Formula. For them, the creeds and theology of the post–New Testament era mark a turn away from the radical centrality of the gospel message and the proclamation of the death and Resurrection of Jesus Christ.[51]

Recovering and Reformulating Chalcedon in the Twentieth Century

The Third Stage in the Quest[52]

For many Roman Catholic and Protestant theologians, the mid- to late-twentieth century marked a dramatic return to Christology and particularly the attempt to root Christological thinking in the historical person and life of Jesus of Nazareth. This process is sometimes referred to as beginning Christology "from below," meaning beginning theology from the life and message of Jesus and then attempting to coordinate this portrait of Jesus with the theological doctrines that emerge in the next five hundred years. Beginning in this way, with an analysis of Jesus' historical ministry and message, fueled a remarkable revival of theology and a process of recovering and reinterpreting the theological tradition formulated at the Council of Chalcedon. This project of reformulation was based on three fundamental elements.

1. A New Understanding of History

A new and more sophisticated view of history leads to what is often termed the "Third Quest for the Historical Jesus." This understanding of history recognizes the role interpretation always plays in human memory; as a result, all historical accounts of people and events are imbued with layers of interpretation

---

51. See Galvin, "Jesus Christ," 282–87.

52. See Marcus Borg, *Meeting Jesus Again for the First Time: The Historical Jesus and the Heart of Contemporary Faith* (San Francisco: Harper, 1995); John Dominic Crossan, *The Historical Jesus: The Life of a Mediterranean Jewish Peasant* (San Francisco: Harper, 1992); Luke Timothy Johnson, *The Real Jesus: The Misguided Quest for the Historical Jesus and the Truth of the Traditional Gospels* (San Francisco: Harper, 1997); J. P. Meier, *A Marginal Jew: Rethinking the Historical Jesus*, vol. 1, *The Roots of the Problem and the Person* (New York: Doubleday, 1991); N. T. Wright, *Jesus and the Victory of God: Christian Origins and the Question of God*, v. 2, 6th ed. (Minneapolis: Fortress, 1997). For a good overview of the current positions, see David B. Gowler, *What Are They Saying about the Historical Jesus?* (Mahwah, NJ: Paulist Press, 2007), and Gelpi, *Encountering Jesus Christ*, 87–108.

and inference. This does not mean the past is inaccessible, but it does mean the past should be approached in a self-critical and self-conscious way. Contemporary historical study always presumes historians cannot fully separate themselves from their own historical context, with its unique set of issues, concerns, and biases. This means all historical analysis, not just that of Jesus, must be critical of its tendency to project the present onto its subject. Such historical analysis, therefore, is cautious about its conclusions. There is a tentative quality to any historical investigation, as it must remain open to revision, clarification, and dialogue with other scholars and future discoveries.

The Third Quest demanded theologians and scripture scholars alike go beyond merely authenticating isolated words and actions of Jesus and instead give an account of Jesus' person and ministry as a whole within the context of first-century Judea, insofar as this cultural context can be reconstructed. This approach led to a gradual elaboration of rational criteria, not only for distinguishing the historical Jesus from the Jesus of faith but also for penetrating his world and that of his followers. These historical criteria established Jesus as a figure like any other ancient figure: there are certain events, characteristics, and sayings that can be attributed to him with a level of certainty and other aspects of his life that are simply out of the reach of critical analysis. Using this method, scholars were tentatively able to assemble three levels of historical development in the New Testament: a portrait of the historical person Jesus of Nazareth and those aspects of the New Testament that might genuinely be ascribed to him; the lives, historical contexts, and beliefs of the first generation of believers that followed him and spread his message in the years between his death and the development of the written texts of the New Testament; and the social context, historical situation, daily practice, and theological perspectives of the authors and their communities, who wrote, edited, or gathered the texts of the New Testament.

2. An Enhanced Understanding of Human Beings

The Enlightenment (1685–1815) began by putting science—rather than God—at the center of reality and therefore focused much of its attention on developing a "humanistic" philosophy that was meant to enhance the progress of human existence. Throughout this period of history however, the understanding of human beings largely remained stagnant. But the twentieth century marked a tremendous surge of interest in penetrating more deeply into the question of what it means to be a human being. With the emergence and rapid advance of fields like medical science, psychology, sociology, and anthropology in the twentieth century, this study made wide advances. Gains in the "human" or social sciences gave theologians a deeper and more nuanced understanding of the human person and human life and its relationship to society than would have been possible even a century before. For Christian scholars, these advances affected not only their understanding of Jesus as a human person but also their understanding of the lives of his followers. The development of the social sciences advanced the understanding of three aspects of human life: (1) the interrelationships that necessarily exist between individuals and communities of people; (2) the process of personal transformation and the stages of growth and development common in human lives; and (3) the effects that experiences like faith, belief, and relationships have on human behavior. These insights greatly enhanced attempts to critically reflect on the past theological tradition and to reinterpret it for a new historical context.

Reflect and Discuss

Consider again the effect of Belle on not only the beast but the whole society in which she lived. Compare the impact of her character on the people she frees to that of Superman. Consider again how the beauty of Belle transforms the beast and both restores him to his original humanity and enhances his life by teaching him how to love.

3. Renewed Theological Focus on the Trinity

The mid-twentieth century saw a profound recovery of theological interest in the Trinity and its significance for all aspects of theology in both Roman Catholic and Protestant circles.[53] These theologians realized that no adequate interpretation of Christian life, including the nature and mission of the church, could take place outside of the divine life and its plan for all of creation revealed in the missions of the Son and the Spirit. In other words, most Christian theologians recovered the belief that all of creation—and especially human life—could only be adequately understood in light of the outpouring of the triune divine love of the Father, Son, and Holy Spirit. This reality had to serve as the starting point, context, and goal of all theological reflection and practical matters concerning the church, moral and ethical judgments, and spirituality. The reality of the Trinity also, therefore, sheds immense light on the reality of Jesus, and he in turn serves not only to reveal but to embody the deepest meaning and reality of the life of God.

A Roman Catholic Example

The new historical method presented by the Third Quest contributed to a dramatic rise in interest in Christology among Roman Catholic scholars in the

---

53. Markey, *Who Is God?*, 74–81.

contemporary period. Countless theologians and Catholic writers have sought to explain the person and message of Jesus Christ by trying to integrate a vivid historical account of Jesus of Nazareth with the long history of Christological reflection that preceded the Enlightenment. One of the most extensive and important examples of this new approach to Christology from the Roman Catholic perspective was produced by the Dutch theologian Edward Schillebeeckx.[54] Over a ten-year period in the 1970s, Schillebeeckx produced two extensive and interconnected works. In the first volume, *Jesus: An Experiment in Christology*,[55] he attempts to offer a thorough, scholarly, and historically complex analysis of the life and ministry of Jesus of Nazareth. He not only seeks to develop a nuanced and viable picture of the historical Jesus but also investigates the effect he had on the lives of his followers. In the second volume, *Christ: The Experience of Jesus as Lord*,[56] Schillebeeckx investigates the historical development of theology as a continual process of attempting to adequately interpret Jesus and the God he reveals. Schillebeeckx considers this theological evolution to be the natural result of the life-changing experience of God's presence in and through the person of Jesus and the ongoing attempt to embody this message in the life of the church. The legacy of the historical Jesus contained in the New Testament represents the church's desire to understand God's salvific self-communication (often termed *grace*) through Jesus of Nazareth.

In both volumes, Schillebeeckx asserts that all divine revelation must be mediated through human experience and that human experience always includes a dimension of interpretation. This means revelation cannot be reduced to merely human experience and that without both experience and its interpretation access to the divine life and communication would be impossible. Therefore, there is simply no complete and fully "objective" access to either the historical life of Jesus or to a final and unmediated interpretation of the God he represents. For Schillebeeckx, this does not diminish the validity of Jesus, his revelation, or the theology that tries to interpret both, but it does place all three of these firmly in the realm of human experience and thus enables them to exert continuing and profound influence in every generation and cultural context.[57]

---

54. Galvin, "Jesus Christ," 307–9.

55. Edward Schillebeeckx, *Jesus: An Experiment in Christology*, trans. Hubert Hoskins (New York: Crossroads, 1979).

56. Edward Schillebeeckx, *Christ: The Experience of Jesus as Lord*, trans. John Bowden (New York: Crossroad, 1980).

57. See Mary Catherine Hilkert, "Discovery of the Living God: Revelation and Experience," in *The Praxis of Christian Experience: An Introduction to the Theology of Edward Schillebeeckx*, ed. Robert J. Schreiter and Mary Catherine Hilkert (San Francisco: Harper & Row, 1989), 35–51.

Two Critical Perspectives on Contemporary Christology

The second half of the twentieth century also saw the emergence of critical theory.[58] Critical theory points out that most social sciences—and especially history—are rooted in false and even dangerous ideologies that prop up systems of dominance and dependence. Critical theory seeks to identify these false ideologies and challenge the assumptions upon which they are based. Critical theory offers an alternative account of the structures of society and the cultural realities that emphasize their tendency to marginalize, diminish, or even exclude the lives and voices of certain people because of gender, race, religion, or social class. Social theorists seek to recover the place and voices of these marginalized peoples, to reinterpret history from their point of view, and to change social structures to include those who have been historically forgotten. Most social theories begin from a "hermeneutic of suspicion," meaning they start interpreting any past event, cultural context, or socioeconomic structure from the suspicion that it has excluded—often violently—many people from sharing in the full benefits of these realities. Critical theory seeks to restore the balance in history and social analysis by telling the story and highlighting the reality of those peoples who have been excluded. Two movements inspired by critical theory that have had the greatest influence on contemporary Christology are liberation theology and feminist theology.

Liberation theology began in Latin America but has come to represent all those who find themselves in a "scandalous condition" in history, the victims of institutional oppression, violence, injustice, and inequity that permeate the world.[59] These theologians critique traditional Christology, even that reformulated in the late twentieth century, for being more interested in the philosophical and theoretical interpretation of Jesus Christ than in his radical and liberating message that God is on the side of the poor and the oppressed. For liberation theologians, Jesus came not just to announce God's saving plan for all humanity, but to put that plan into motion by changing history. Liberation theologians insist theories about God and Jesus cannot be separated from *praxis* (Greek for "action" or "practice"). Correct interpretation of Jesus (orthodoxy) means interpreting the implications of his life and message and living out his call to directly serve those in need and transforming the negative and scandalous social structures (including religions) that ruin their lives. Liberation theologians insist Jesus Christ reveals God is the God of life, liberation, and justice, and that

---

58. See Stephen Eric Bonner, *Critical Theory: A Very Short Introduction* (Oxford: Oxford University Press, 2011); Markey, *Who Is God?*, 81.

59. For a short history and explanation of liberation theology, see Roberto Oliveros, "History and Theology of Liberation," in *Mysterium Liberationis: Fundamental Concepts of Liberation Theology*, ed. Ignacio Ellacuria and Jon Sobrino (Maryknoll, NY: Orbis, 1993), 3–32.

theologians must not only affirm this truth but enable and develop strategies to put this truth into action.[60]

This emphasis on critique and direct personal and social action challenges academic theologians and churches to "close the loop" between thinking about history and working to change it. These theologians insist that what is acknowledged as orthodox faith necessarily include an ethical and sociopolitical response (called *orthopraxis*, meaning "right action") to the abstract formulas handed down from the Councils of Nicea and Chalcedon. This requires that theologians consider not just the impact of Jesus Christ for individual personal salvation but also the social, political, and economic implications of his life and message. The results of social theory and structural analyses of the sources of injustice and oppression are not just adjunct or secondary dimensions of faith; they are central to understanding and rightly interpreting Jesus Christ.

Reflect and Discuss

Think about the ways in which Jean Vanier and the L'Arche community "close the gap" between theory and practice in the ways they live out the Christian message. How might this be an example of the sort of right action that liberation theology demands?

Feminist theology, a very significant type of liberation theology, insists that the hermeneutic of suspicion needs to be applied to historical analysis especially in regard to the treatment of women and the subjugation and silencing of women throughout history. Feminist Roman Catholic theologian Elizabeth Johnson describes the method of all liberation theology as having three steps: (1) analyzing the situation of injustice and oppression, (2) searching the tradition (history) for the contributing causes of this oppression, and (3) searching history and tradition again for often overlooked or misinterpreted aspects of the tradition that bring liberation and new life.[61]

Following this model, Christian feminist theologians begin by attempting to expose the corrosive effects of sexism in the Christian tradition. Sexism is an ideology that considers males to be intellectually and morally superior to females. Sexism maintains that this superiority is not merely a cultural or historical accident but is ordained by nature. The fundamental subjugation and

---

60. See Gustavo Gutierrez, *The God of Life*, trans. Mathew J. O'Connell (Maryknoll, NY: Orbis, 1991), and Julio Lois, "Christology in the Theology of Liberation," in *Mysterium Liberationis*, ed. Ellacuria and Sobrino, 168–93.

61. Elizabeth A. Johnson, *Consider Jesus: Waves of Renewal in Christology* (New York: Crossroad, 1990), 99.

oppression of women throughout history in almost all cultural contexts largely rests on this ideology. Feminists seek not only to refute this ideology but to discover and investigate the often hidden yet extensive ways that it shapes cultural assumptions about reality, knowledge, society, and even God. Catholic feminist theologians have been particularly concerned about the ways that sexism shapes most people's perceptions of God and the images they associate with the divine life.[62]

Second, feminist theologians insist that language about God and symbols of God often hide or disguise the reality of women and their equal participation in the divine life and plan. The equality of all people before God is often concealed rather than revealed by constant use of the same sexist language to refer to God. To use male language exclusively to describe God, especially male pronouns ("he," "him," and "his"), is to conceal the rich and profound possibilities of human imagination to contemplate and articulate the mystery of triune life. God can be referred to in myriad ways and Scripture itself uses a vast number of analogies to refer to the mystery of God and God's profound compassion for all human beings. To limit all language of God to a few terms and pronouns ultimately diminishes not just the very people God came to save, but denies God the glory only a flourishing of images can bestow.

Finally, feminist theologians discover in the Gospels striking and systematic examples of Jesus being profoundly inclusive of women. He called women to be his disciples, included them in his ministry, stayed and ate in their homes, and depended upon them to support him and his ministry financially (Luke 8:1–3). Women followed him on his final trip to Jerusalem, refused to betray him when the male disciples ran away, surrounded him at his death, and were the first to discover the Resurrection and announce it to others. Women were filled with the Holy Spirit after the Resurrection and were sent to preach the gospel and share in the ministry of the early church.[63] Elizabeth Johnson notes that at some points the New Testament identifies Jesus with the Wisdom of God (1 Cor. 1:24), which had been personified in the book of Wisdom as Lady Wisdom.[64] That Jesus is the presence of the Wisdom of God indicates that, after the Resurrection, Christ is neither male nor female (Gal. 3:28) but only fully represented by the whole community of believers inclusive of all their differences. Feminist theologians recover these lost or marginalized examples of the presence of women in the life of Jesus as a foundational part of the post-Resurrection community of disciples and employ them to develop a richer and more complete portrait of the historical Jesus and the theological investigation of his life and message.

---

62. For a good, brief description of Christian feminist theology, see Elizabeth A. Johnson, *She Who Is: The Mystery of God in Feminist Theological Discourse* (New York: Crossroad, 1992), 22–33.

63. Johnson, *Consider Jesus*, 108–10.

64. Johnson, *She Who Is*, 86–90. See Prov. 1:20–33; 4:13; 8; 9:1–6; Sir. 24:19–23.

Reflect and Discuss

Is there something about Belle as a person and as a woman that makes her particularly suitable as a Christ-figure? Does the gender of a person alter or hinder how they can represent Christ? Is there anyone in your life that you would consider Christ-like after reading these chapters? What is it about them that makes you think of Jesus Christ?

Review Questions

1. List some of the challenges Hellenistic culture posed to early Christian beliefs about who Jesus was.
2. Identify and briefly describe the two early, problematic patterns of explaining the relationship between Jesus' humanity and divinity.
3. What beliefs about Jesus does the Nicene Creed affirm?
4. How does the Chalcedonian Creed help explain the relationship between Jesus' humanity and divinity?
5. What are some of the reasons medieval and scholastic theologians gave for God becoming human in the person of Jesus?
6. What was the major shift in many Enlightenment interpretations of Jesus?
7. Why did Enlightenment thinkers make a distinction between the "Jesus of history" and the "Christ of faith"?
8. In the nineteenth century, what was the primary outcome of the Quest for the Historical Jesus?
9. What three elements shaped the Third Quest for the Historical Jesus?
10. What is liberation theology's critique of traditional doctrinal Christology?
11. According to feminist theology, what is the starting point for all theology, including Christology?

Discussion Questions

1. Why were the early Christian theologians so concerned to explain how Jesus was both human and divine? Do these concerns seem important to you? Why, or why not?
2. Why were medieval and scholastic theologians so concerned to explain why Jesus died and rose again?

3. In your opinion, is the historical life of Jesus necessary for Christian faith? Is faith in Christ's life, death, and Resurrection possible without proof of their historical validity? How do you understand the relationship between the Jesus of history and the Christ of faith?

4. What aspects of contemporary culture (if any) are critical of Christian faith, and what aspects (if any) support Christian faith?

5. Of the major questions asked by patristic, medieval, Enlightenment, and contemporary theologians about Jesus, which ones do you find the most intriguing?

6. What new questions about the life and significance of Jesus do you think might emerge in the future?

Additional Resources

PRINT

Dunn, James D. G. *The Christ and the Spirit.* Vol. 1, *Christology.* 2 vols. Grand Rapids: Eerdmans, 1998.

Endō, Shūsaku. *A Life of Jesus.* New York: Paulist Press, 1978.

Gelpi, Donald L. *Encountering Jesus Christ: Rethinking Christological Faith and Commitment.* Marquette Studies in Theology 65. Milwaukee: Marquette University Press, 2009.

Grant, Jaquelyn. *White Women's Christ and Black Women's Jesus: Feminist Christology and Womanist Response.* AAR Academy Series 64. Atlanta: Scholars Press, 1989.

Gutierrez, Gustavo. *A Theology of Liberation: History, Politics, and Salvation.* Rev. ed. Maryknoll, NY: Orbis, 1988.

Hopkins, Julie M. *Towards a Feminist Christology: Jesus of Nazareth, European Women, and the Christological Crisis.* Grand Rapids: Eerdmans, 1995.

Isherwood, Lisa. *Introducing Feminist Christologies (Introductions in Feminist Theology).* 1st ed. Sheffield, UK: Sheffield Academic Press, 2002.

Johnson, Elizabeth A. *Consider Jesus: Waves of Renewal in Christology.* New York: Crossroad, 1990.

Johnson, Luke Timothy. *Living Jesus: Learning the Heart of the Gospel.* Reprint ed. San Francisco: HarperOne, 2000.

―――. *The Writings of the New Testament.* 3rd ed. Minneapolis: Fortress, 2010.

Kasper, Walter. *The God of Jesus Christ.* New York: Crossroad, 1984.

Loewe, William P. *The College Student's Introduction to Christology* (Wilmington, DE: Michael Glazier, 1996).

McMahon, Christopher. *Understanding Jesus: Christology from Emmaus to Today*. Rev. ed. Winona, MN: Anselm Academic, 2013.

Moltmann, Jurgen. *The Coming of God: Christian Eschatology*. Minneapolis: Fortress, 2004.

———. *The Crucified God: The Cross of Christ as the Foundation and Criticism of Christian Theology*. 1st Fortress Press ed. Minneapolis: Fortress, 1993.

Nolan, Albert. *Jesus before Christianity*. Rev. ed. Maryknoll, N.Y: Orbis, 1992.

Pedraja, Luis G. *Jesus Is My Uncle: Christology from a Hispanic Perspective*. Nashville: Abingdon, 1999.

Power, David Noel. *Love without Calculation: A Reflection on Divine Kenosis; "He Emptied Himself, Taking the Form of a Slave," Philippians 2:7*. New York: Crossroad, 2005.

Stevens, Maryanne, ed. *Reconstructing the Christ Symbol: Essays in Feminist Christology*. Eugene, OR: Wipf & Stock, 2004.

Tanner, Norman. *The Councils of the Church: A Short History*. New York: Crossroad, 2001.

Witherington, Ben. *The Christology of Jesus*. Minneapolis: Fortress, 1990.

Wright, N. T. *The Challenge of Jesus: Rediscovering Who Jesus Was and Is*. Downer's Grove, IL: IVP Books, 2015.

OTHER MEDIA

Wright, N. T. NTWrightPage. *http://ntwrightpage.com/category/audio-video/*. Video of lectures on Christology by N. T. Wright.

Ryan, Robin, CP. *A Retreat with Jesus Christ*. DVD, CD, and MP3 file. Now You Know Media, 2017. Lectures by Robin Ryan, CP.

Ryan, Robin, CP. *Christology: Understanding Jesus*. DVD, CD, and MP3 file. Now You Know Media, 2017. Lectures by Robin Ryan, CP.

The Holy Spirit: The Giver of Life[1]

The Christian understanding of the Holy Spirit is, in many ways, a work in progress. The present chapter attempts to set out key features of the Christian idea of the Spirit, how it came about, and how it continues to develop. The writings of the New Testament, especially the epistles of Paul and the Gospel of John, have proved crucial in this unfolding story, but the idea of God's Spirit is much older. The story begins with the Hebrew Scriptures.

The Holy Spirit in the Hebrew Scriptures

The Hebrew word for "spirit" (*ruah*) occurs 378 times in the Hebrew Scriptures. It is always used in one of three ways.[2] First, *ruah* literally means "breath" or "breathing into," and connotes a life source that can be transmitted to something or someone. Second, it can refer to a strong, rushing, desert wind that carries a great deal of force or power. Third, it indicates the presence of God in the world in a direct and personal way as a force, power, or relationship, particularly in human lives.

In the first chapters of the book of Genesis, all of these aspects of the term are present. In Genesis 1:2, the *ruah* of God is "sweeping over the waters" of chaos and darkness out of which God creates the heavens and earth in seven days. In Genesis 2:7, God creates a human from the soil of the earth and *breathes* life into it; this in turn causes the person to come to life and

---

1. Portions of this chapter are adapted from John J. Markey, *Creating Communion: The Theology of the Constitutions of the Church* (New York: New City, 2004), particularly 103–26, used with permission.

2. Yves Congar, *I Believe in the Holy Spirit*, trans. David Smith (New York: Seabury, 1983), 1:3.

begin *breathing*. So the divine *ruah* serves as both an agent and catalyst of the whole of creation and as a special and profoundly intimate link between human beings and God. Throughout the Hebrew Scriptures, the divine *ruah* acts in all three ways: the *ruah* of God serves as a transformative force at work in the world and as a personal link to the divine life empowering new religious consciousness, authentic prophecy, and creative interpretation of the will of God.[3]

Second-century statue personifying Wisdom (from the ancient Greek *Sophia*). Wisdom was a central concept of Hellenistic philosophy and culture. From the Celsus Library in Ephesus.

The general understanding of *ruah* in the Hebrew Scriptures comes to a unique fulfillment in the wisdom literature. In these works, the idea of wisdom borrowed from the Greek culture (*sophia*) is basically identified with *ruah*, for it seems to have the same action and effect.[4] Here wisdom—often personified as a woman (Lady Wisdom)—helps human beings penetrate to the heart of things, opening the complexity and mystery of life to those who trust and follow her. Entering into a relationship with Lady Wisdom offers the person new vision and a new critical frame of reference from which to judge reality more genuinely and truly. This suggests that the relationship with the *ruah*, like that with Lady Wisdom, is a profoundly intimate and transformative experience that brings the person into a higher level of conscious awareness about the world and his or her relationship with God. The personification of wisdom as a woman also provides the first real personal biblical imagery speaking about the *ruah*: that of a beautiful and wise woman mentor who attracts us and guides people into ever-deeper realms of knowledge and love.

---

3. Donald Gelpi, *The Spirit in the World*, Zacchaeus Studies: Theology (Wilmington, DE: Michael Glazier, 1988), 5–15.

4. Congar, *I Believe in the Holy Spirit*, 1:9–12. For the Holy Spirit in general, see Donald Gelpi, *The Divine Mother: A Trinitarian Theology of the Holy Spirit* (Lanham, MD: University Press of America, 1984).

The Holy Spirit in the New Testament

In the New Testament the term *pneuma* is the Greek equivalent or translation of *ruah*; the use of the term *ruah* in the Hebrew Scriptures sets the context and helps to interpret the term *pneuma*. In the Synoptic Gospels (Matthew, Mark, and Luke), Jesus is always depicted as the one with the fullness of the *pneuma* and the one who shares his *pneuma* with his disciples after his death and Resurrection.[5] Jesus' life is not seen as separate from the divine *pneuma*, nor vice versa. But in all the narrative accounts of the life of Jesus, his life represents or signifies what human life can look like when it is open completely to the transforming power of the *pneuma*. The Gospels are written later than the Pauline epistles (as explained earlier) and serve as an attempt to remember the life and teaching of Jesus in light of the passion, death, and Resurrection of Jesus, and his bestowing of the Holy Spirit upon his disciples, which is the true center of each Gospel proclamation. The Pauline texts, written explicitly in reference to the paschal mystery, offer the most complete understanding of the theology of the Holy Spirit (called *pneumatolgy*) in the New Testament. Similarly, the Acts of the Apostles, as a record of the *pneuma*'s work in building up the body of Christ (or the church), as the final stage of the paschal mystery, gives witness to the unique pattern of the *pneuma*'s "working relationship" with the Christian communities.

Pneuma in Paul[6]

Paul has a privileged place among New Testament writers for two reasons: Paul is probably the only New Testament writer who could claim to have personally seen the risen Christ, and he reflected in considerable detail about the theological significance of Jesus' Resurrection in the light of his own experience and in the light of the experience of others that was directly communicated to him. Paul's theological vision unfolds pastorally rather than systematically in his surviving letters. Nevertheless, Paul demonstrates a remarkable level of coherence in his religious vision and understanding of the meaning of Jesus Christ and the paschal mystery. Paul's pneumatology, therefore, arose in tandem with his Christology as a response to specific doctrinal and pastoral problems that developed in the communities he founded.

One of the earliest and most significant texts of Christological and pneumatological importance is 1 Corinthians 15. This text evidently developed to address the doubts of some members of the Corinthian community regarding

---

5. Gelpi, *The Spirit in the World*, 15–53.

6. Terrence Paige, "Holy Spirit," in *Dictionary of Paul and His Letters*, ed. Gerald F. Hawthorne, Ralph Martin, and Daniel G Reid (Downers Grove, IL: InterVarsity, 1993), 404–13; Luke Timothy Johnson, *The Writings of the New Testament*, 3rd ed. (Minneapolis: Fortress, 2010), 227–403.

Christ's bodily Resurrection. Paul responds that Jesus not only died but was buried and that he rose and "appeared to Cephas, then to the Twelve. After that, he appeared to more than five hundred brothers at once" (vv. 5–6). "Last of all," he appeared to Paul (v. 8). This means that Jesus' Resurrection was not a private encounter or revelation shared by only a few people but represents the shared faith and shared experience of the first community of Christians. It is this experience that authenticates the good news they proclaim, and their specific claims about the bodily Resurrection. Any doubts, therefore, about the Resurrection directly contradict the shared faith of the rest of the apostolic community of faith. Paul goes on to develop in the rest of this text a dynamic and complex picture of Jesus' Resurrection.

In this context, Paul makes what at first seems like an astonishing claim: through the Resurrection, Jesus has become "a life-giving Spirit [*pneuma*]" (1 Cor. 15:45). This assertion implies that Jesus' personal transformation in the *pneuma* culminated in the Resurrection, because it transformed him totally, making his physical body into a *pneumatic* (spiritual) body capable of an imperishable and heavenly mode of existence. This also reveals that there is both a vital and functional identity of life between the risen Christ and the *pneuma* of God. It is vital because the Christ shares fully in the divine *pneumatic* life in a unique and distinct way that implies both are equally part of God's single plan for salvation. There is a functional identity because both act in ways that are "life-giving" and sanctifying for those who put their faith in God's saving power acting through the paschal mystery.

This same reasoning is seen in 2 Corinthians 3:15–18. Paul refers to the risen Christ in relation to the *pneuma*: "Now the Lord is the Spirit (*pneuma*), and where the Spirit (*pneuma*) of the Lord is, there is freedom. All of us, gazing with unveiled face on the glory of the Lord, are being transformed into the same image from glory to glory, as from the Lord who is the Spirit (*pneuma*)." Paul seems to be claiming there is a *functional identity* between Jesus and the *pneuma* such that wherever the *pneuma* of God is present and acting, the risen Christ is also present and acting. Whoever possesses the *pneuma* of God possess the risen life of Christ as well. The *pneuma* of God transforms believers into the "image" of Christ, reflecting his glory; seeing with "unveiled face" the glory of Christ revealing the divine reality. These believers are growing "from glory to glory" meaning the Resurrection offers progressive and intensive growth and transformation in the *pneuma*. The new life initiated by the paschal mystery is a historical process that continues through the power of the *pneuma* grounded in the vital identity of life shared by the *pneuma* and the risen Christ.

Throughout the New Testament, the *pneuma* functions as the divine principle of empowering, saving enlightenment. By asserting a vital functional identity between the risen Christ and the divine *pneuma*, Paul is claiming that in the encounter with the risen Lord one receives the Spirit in an utterly powerful and transforming way, and vice versa. This experience gives believers the authority and the hope to testify to the saving power of the Resurrection. It also means a personal encounter with the Spirit connects one directly with the death and Resurrection of Jesus and allows them to share in their effects. Paul then offers a view of the work of the *pneuma* that is liberating, not controlling; cooperative, not overpowering. The *pneuma* helps one not only to see, but to desire to see God.

Reflect and Discuss

Compare the role that beauty plays in Belle's story with that of the *pneuma* in Paul's writings. In what ways does beauty transform, enlighten, and empower people in the story of *Beauty and the Beast*?

This understanding of the paschal mystery is brought to a kind of systematic presentation in Paul's Letter to the Romans. Throughout this text, Paul reflects on the saving mystery of Christ's death and Resurrection and its practical implications for believers and all of humanity. This reflection comes to a crescendo in chapter 8:9–17.[7] Paul presents an understanding of human existence transformed through the paschal mystery in the power of the *pneuma* that can only be described as a mutual indwelling: Christians in Christ, Christ in Christians, Christians in the *pneuma*, the *pneuma* in Christians. Through the *pneuma*, human beings come to participate in the risen Christ by receiving a share in his risen life. This "pneumatic" transformation enables righteous living that manifests God's presence. It also gives believers a new history in that they take on the story of Christ himself in such a way that Christ's story becomes their story and his relationships become their relationships. This means disciples enter into the family of God in a radically new way, a way that gives them direct access to the Father and unites them with all of the rest of God's children who have been adopted in Christ. The pneumatic transformation the individual experiences has essentially social and communal consequences in that it incorporates one into the body of Christ[8] and the family of God. The mutual indwelling affected by this transformation implies an added indwelling of Christians in one another.

The implications of the social and communal dimensions of pneumatic transformation are most thoroughly explored by Paul in Romans 12–14 and in

---

7. Johnson, *The Writings of the New Testament*, 315.

8. The body of Christ here refers to the church; see Markey, *Creating Communion*, 126.

1 Corinthians 12. In both instances, Paul examines the Christian community in terms of the interrelationships between the parts of a body. In both he insists the fullness of the *pneuma* can only be experienced in community, and never in some kind of mystical isolation. The *pneuma* builds up the community through what Paul calls *charismata*: gracious gifts that are particular instances of *charis*, God's saving activity (grace). The interrelating and mutual sharing of these *charismata* make community possible and the *pneuma* fully manifest. The *pneuma's* manifestation is ultimately the manifestation of the presence of Christ; it is the sharing of the *charismata* that makes disciples into the body of Christ. Furthermore, the *pneuma* links up each community with other communities of faith in the worldwide body of Christ. In the end of Romans 8, Paul explains how the *pneuma* then connects each community into the universal community, and ultimately ties the whole universe into the life of God.

A final important dimension of Paul's understanding of the unique mission of the divine *pneuma* is revealed in 1 Corinthians 2:10–16:

For the Spirit (*pneuma*) scrutinizes everything, even the depths God. Among human beings, who knows what pertains to a person except the spirit of the person that is within? Similarly, no one knows what pertains to God except the Spirit of God. We have not received the spirit of the world but the Spirit that is from God, so that we may understand the things freely given us by God. And we speak about them not with words taught by human wisdom, but with words taught by the Spirit, describing spiritual realities in spiritual terms. Now the natural person does not accept what pertains to the Spirit of God, for to him it is foolishness, and he cannot understand it, because it is judged spiritually. The spiritual person, however, can judge everything but is not subject to judgment by anyone. For "who has known the mind of the Lord, so as to counsel him?" But we have the mind of Christ.

For Paul, the *pneuma* is the very mind of God; to be personally transformed in and enlightened by the *pneuma*, therefore, is to be drawn into the divine life in a totally unique and extraordinary way. In the power of the *pneuma*, people know the depths of their own consciousness, and also envision God's saving intention for all humanity. The fruit of this type of knowledge is hope and complete trust in God's providence (as opposed to skepticism and fear), which allows transformed persons to see the world as God sees it and make sound judgments about their lives and ethical choices. Jesus incarnates the mind of God; he is the spoken Word that gives concrete knowledge of what one needs to know about God and God's plan for the world. The *pneuma*, as the mind of God, transforms Christians so that they can take on the mind of Christ and thereby serve the plan of God as an ongoing part of Jesus Christ's own life and mission.

The Holy Spirit in the Gospel of Luke and Acts of the Apostles

It is generally assumed that the Gospel of Luke and the Acts of the Apostles were written by the same author.[9] But the author or authors, the communities being addressed, and the dates of composition all remain uncertain.[10] The author uses about 60 percent of Mark's Gospel and clearly wrote after the destruction of Jerusalem (70 CE), so many scholars estimate the Gospel of Luke and the book of Acts were written in the early 80s, for a community of mostly Gentile Christians. But one can only guess where this community was located.

Nevertheless, it is possible to infer a great deal about Luke's intention in writing his two volumes. The first volume recounts Jesus' proclamation of the kingdom, and the second volume recounts the Christian community's proclamation of the risen Christ. The first volume is about the life, message, death, and Resurrection of Jesus Christ; the second volume is about the coming of the *pneuma* and its life and activity through the Christian community.[11]

Luke frequently invokes the theme of "fulfillment," but for him it implies not just Jesus as the fulfillment of salvation history as revealed in the Jewish tradition but also the fulfillment of Jesus' work to bring the good news of salvation to the Gentiles and to the ends of the earth. The movement of Jesus from Galilee to Jerusalem in the first volume has a parallel in the movement of the proclamation from Jerusalem to Rome in the second volume. The journey of the Christian community from the small region of Palestine throughout the Roman Empire signals the birth and expansion of the gospel throughout the world with the Resurrection and the sending of the *pneuma*.

The Acts of the Apostles begins with the disciples in Jerusalem after the Resurrection, awaiting God's call to send them out to preach the good news of the risen Christ. The disciples are gathered together for the Jewish Festival of Weeks, or Pentecost (Acts 2). In the Jewish tradition, the Pentecost festival took place fifty days after Passover and traditionally marked the day the law was given to Israel by Moses.[12] The Holy Spirit descends upon the disciples and empowers them to go forward and proclaim the good news in dramatic and bold ways. In the book of Acts, the initial Pentecost event leads to a series of "pentecosts," narrative accounts of the sending and manifestation of the *pneuma*. Each such occurrence consists of three interrelated events: (1) the reception of the *pneuma* transforms and conforms the community into the image of Christ, (2) this community is immediately sent out to preach the

9. Johnson, *The Writings of the New Testament*, 187–225, see also James D. G. Dunn, *The Christ and The Spirit* (Grand Rapids: Eerdmans, 1998), 205–42.

10. Johnson, *The Writings of the New Testament*, 187–90.

11. Ibid., 196.

12. John Kaltner and Steven L. McKenzie, *The Back Door Introduction to the Bible* (Winona, MN: Anselm Academic, 2012), 137.

The Walters Art Museum, Purchased by Henry Walters, after 1902

Depiction of the scene described in Acts 2:1–5: "they were all together in one place. And suddenly from heaven there came a sound like the rush of a violent wind. . . . Divided tongues, as of fire, appeared among them, and a tongue rested on each of them. All of them were filled with the Holy Spirit."

gospel to others, which (3) transforms them and welcomes them into the community, which is portrayed as a common life centered around the new morality of Christ. The new community is meant to conform to the image of Christ. In other words, it is meant to become Christ's body.

For the author of Luke/Acts, the immediate response to hearing the word through preaching and the subsequent experience of the transformative power of the *pneuma*, is the formation of a radically new community (Acts 2:42–47; 4:32–35). This community is characterized by a radical sharing of life and goods and reaches its fullness in the sharing of one heart and mind. The *pneuma* is mediated through the witness of others—especially through a transformed community—but is always personally experienced as well. Once experienced, the *pneuma* draws the individual into the community of believers that is the body of Christ.

Reflect and Discuss

Do you see any connections or parallels between the L'Arche community and the type of Spirit-transformed community that is described above?

Pneuma and *Paraklētos* in the Gospel of John

In John's Gospel, the *pneuma* inspires authentic worship of God and is the source of the divine enlightenment that guides the disciples of Jesus in faithful witness to his Resurrection.[13] John also introduces the term *paraklētos* ("helper" or "advocate") to refer to the *pneuma* in the last discourse of Jesus. This is the only place in the whole of the New Testament where this term appears.

---

13. Gelpi, *The Divine Mother*, 55–56. See also Congar, *I Believe in the Holy Spirit*, 1:49–56; Johnson, *The Writings of the New Testament*, 461–524.

In two central texts early in the Gospel, Jesus refers to the essentially pneumatic character of all authentic worship of God. To Nicodemus's inquiry about the possibility of being born a second time, Jesus answers, "No one can enter the kingdom of God without being born of water and Spirit. What is born of flesh is flesh and what is born of spirit is spirit" (3:5–6). Later, to the Samaritan woman, Jesus proclaims,

> But the hour is coming, and is now here, when true worshipers will worship the Father in Spirit (*pneuma*) and truth; and indeed the Father seeks such people to worship him. God is Spirit (*pneuma*), and those who worship him must worship in Spirit (*pneuma*) and truth. (4:23–24)

These texts dramatically imply that the *pneuma* designates a central reality in which both the Father and Jesus participate. To be reborn in the *pneuma* or to worship "in" the *pneuma* is to enter fully into the very mystery of God's own life revealed in Christ. To truly worship as Christ does is to see the face of the Father and to gain the wisdom of God. Jesus demonstrates this through his life, ministry, message, and Passion. Jesus is "the way and the truth and the life" (14:6); the *pneuma* makes his saving way, truth, and life available to all who are open to the transforming power of the *pneuma*. Once one has this saving transformation, all other forms of institutional religion are rendered secondary to and at the service of authentic Christian worship.

The identification of the *pneuma* as the principle of life of the Godhead also explains why Jesus continually refers to the *pneuma* as the principle of new life for his disciples. Jesus comes to offer new life, and those who want this new life will be given it through his own flesh and blood and his *pneuma*, which together are the source of all life (see particularly John 6). John alludes to this basic formula throughout the Gospel and makes it the foundation of the Eucharistic theology and allusions that run throughout the text. To share in Christ's life is to share in the divine life itself in a direct way in John's Gospel.

In his last discourse, Jesus promises he will send a *paraklētos* after he is gone to confirm the faith of the disciples and to guide them in their post-Resurrection mission (John 14:16–19). The term *paraklētos* has a rich variety of meanings and connotations.[14] Most commonly, however, it is interpreted in legal or forensic terms. In this sense, the *paraklētos* that Jesus will send is understood to be both an attorney who will convict the world of its guilt in rejecting Jesus and an advocate and witness who will come to testify with and on behalf of the disciples of Jesus who remain true to him. The activity of the *paraklētos* will be to stand by, encourage, and strengthen those who proclaim Jesus as the risen Christ.

The *paraklētos* will also teach and guide the disciples by instructing them in the light of the Resurrection concerning what they must now say and do in

---

14. Gelpi, *The Spirit in the World*, 49–51.

the name of Jesus. Jesus promises he will send "another Advocate (*paraklētos*)" (14:16), implying that Jesus himself is the first *paraklētos*. The second *paraklētos* will continue the work of Jesus, teach the disciples as Jesus himself has done, and conform them to his own likeness. John's Jesus realizes that he cannot teach his disciples all they need to know during his lifetime, because they are unable to hear and understand it. At the end of his life, he promises them that they will receive another *paraklētos*—this time his own *pneuma*—that will teach them all truth and lead them in the ways of divine wisdom. This truth and wisdom is the same as that which the *pneuma* receives from and shares with Jesus so that the disciples receive what Jesus has learned from the Father. The *pneuma* (*paraklētos*), therefore, enlightens the disciples after the Resurrection of Christ with his own knowledge of the divine truth, learned from the Father. This suggests that, for John, the *pneuma* functions as the source of interaction between the Father and the Son. Similarly, human beings who experience the transforming power of the *pneuma* enter into a special relationship with the *pneuma*, the Son, and the Father.[15] This relationship is identified as the new life Jesus came to bring and the salvation he promised to all believers throughout John's Gospel.

Star Wars: Interpreting the Force

"May the Force be with You. . . ."

George Lucas's *Star Wars* saga began "a long time ago in a galaxy far, far away" with *Episode IV: A New Hope* in 1977 and has now spanned over four decades with nine feature-length blockbuster movies, several animated television series, video games, novels, comics, and short stories, which make up the official "canon." This saga chronicles an epic struggle between good and evil represented by two primary opposing forces, the Jedi and the Sith. In addition to the *Star Wars* canon, there are dozens of spin-off books and other media that incorporate many of the central characters and themes of the central saga.

In the *Star Wars* universe, both the Jedi and their mortal enemies, the Sith, rely on a mysterious transcendent power called "the force." The force, as we learn in *Episode IV*, is an energy field that connects all living things to one another. The power of the Jedi and Sith comes through their dedication to learning the ways of the force to manipulate the world around them. The force carries with it a significant and explicit religious

Continued

---

15. See John Markey, *Who Is God? Catholic Perspectives through the Ages* (Winona, MN: Anselm Academic, 2016), 31.

STAR WARS: INTERPRETING THE FORCE Continued

Darth Vader fighting with Obi-Wan Kenobi in *Star Wars Episode IV: A New Hope.*

dimension. The Sith and the Jedi devote their entire lives to training in the ways of the force in monastic-style communities. The Jedi are devoted to "the light" side of the force and seek to use the power of the force to bring balance, harmony, and peace to the galaxy. The Sith, on the other hand, follow the "dark side" of the force and seek to use the force to gain and wield tyrannical power over the galaxy.

The religious dimensions of the force mirror certain aspects of two major world religions, specifically Christianity and Buddhism. In its overall thrust, perhaps the force is closer to the nontheistic nature of the Buddhist tradition, but there are several important parallels to traditional Christian notions of God, particularly the Holy Spirit. First, both the force and the Holy Spirit are presented as primarily spiritual realities, although the force does have a physical dimension in the microscopic cells called *midichlorians* that live in every living thing. Second, both have a vital and active presence in the world and in some sense communicate with people and participate in their daily lives. Additionally, both the Spirit and the force are a source of spiritual vibrancy and strength that can be developed and cultivated through a life of devotion, training, and obedience. And lastly, both the force and the Spirit exist independently of any individual or group's interaction with them. That is, although both the Spirit and the force are dynamic realities in the world

Continued

STAR WARS: INTERPRETING THE FORCE Continued

and may be engaged by people, neither are limited to these engagements and thus exist with a life and nature that is their own.

However, the force and the Holy Spirit of the Christian tradition should not be naively conflated. The Holy Spirit, as a member of the Trinity, is a supremely personal reality with a specific and unique set of traits, characteristics, and a fully-formed will rooted in love. The force, on the other hand is an impersonal and morally ambivalent reality that can be manipulated by and conformed to any person's desire and will. The Holy Spirit cannot be coerced or manipulated by anyone. The Spirit's character is derived from God, for the Spirit is equal to and identified with God, according to the third article of the Nicene Creed.

Moreover, the Holy Spirit, unlike the force, does not possess anything related to the "dark side." The force is an inherently dualistic reality that gives rise to the oppositional forces of the Sith and the Jedi. In the Christian tradition, God in his entirety as Father, Son, and Holy Spirit, is supremely and perfectly good and thus is engaged in the good of his creation. The force, while perhaps mirroring God in its creative energy, is also the author of evil, suffering, hatred, and jealousy, none of which may be accurately said of the Father, Son, and Holy Spirit in Christian orthodoxy. Although there are dualistic tendencies within the Christian tradition that envision demonic spiritual realties (like the devil or Satan) in mortal combat with God and the church, Christian orthodoxy never elevated such evil realities or forces to a level equal in power with God. The force, on the other hand, may be equally effective for the light or dark side, and at points in the saga, the dark side seems to be winning.

The third and perhaps most important difference is the force does not promise or seem even to be interested in offering salvation and deliverance from evil, something that is at the core of God's redemptive relationship with humanity, the world, and the universe at large.

Due to the explicit use of religious themes in the *Star Wars* universe, it is tempting to see the Spirit and the force as similar realities. Though there are several points of contact and thought-provoking parallels between them, there are serious points of departure as well.[16]

---

16. For more on the relationship between *Star Wars* and Christianity, see John C. McDowell, "'Feeling The Force'—Star Wars and Spiritual Truth," Bethinking, *https://www.bethinking.org/culture/feeling-the-force-star-wars-and-spiritual-truth*; Michael Haldas, "The Force, The Holy Spirit and Star Wars," Sacramental Living: Understanding Christianity as a Way of Life, January 5, 2016, *https://www.ancientfaith.com/podcasts/sacramental/starwars*; Joel Hodge, "How 'Star Wars' Answers Our Biggest Religious Questions," *Washington Post*, April 21, 2015, *https://www.washingtonpost.com/postevery thing/wp/2015/04/21/how-star-wars-answers-our-biggest-religious-questions/*; and John C. McDowell, *The Gospel according to Star Wars: Faith, Hope, and the Force* (Louisville: Westminster John Knox, 2007).

Pneumatology in the Theological Tradition

In the period after the New Testament, the theology of Holy Spirit developed in tandem with the Christian understanding of God. One of the most consistent proclamations of the whole of Scripture is that God is love. Christians believe that, purely out of love, God chose to contact human beings and relate to them by inviting them into a saving and eternal relationship with God. God chooses to interact with humanity and accept the consequences of humanity's choices. Similarly, each person can choose to interact with God—or not to interact with God—and accept the consequences. Whatever choice is made will profoundly affect the life of the person and will determine not only the events of one's life but the meaning and purpose of those events.

The Holy Spirit and the Trinity

Christians also believe that God reveals Godself through Jesus Christ as a tri-une community of persons, referred to as the Trinity.[17] The Trinity is primarily known to humans by its effects in history: creation, redemption, and sanctification. These effects actually comprise the Trinity's mission, God's own self-motivated and directed desire to create, relate to, and save human beings and all creation. Trinity means there is not just one monolithic God that acts in a variety of ways, but a single dynamic reality composed of distinct persons (usually termed Father, Son, and Spirit); God is understood as a divine community. Human beings participate in this divine community in creation and in the direct presence of God in each human life. People imitate and share in this reality through their community and social life in imitation of Jesus Christ. Jesus Christ is the incarnate, historical presence of this reality: one person of this divine community, whose mission was to become a divine human person to ensure the salvation of all. Jesus Christ comes to participate directly in historical reality and proclaim and demonstrate God's view of the world and its destiny. Jesus also comes to give every person the Spirit and inaugurate a new dimension of the Spirit's mission. The Spirit no longer acts in general on behalf of God, but actually unites human beings as Christ and gives them the mind of Jesus Christ and puts them in the same relationship with the Father that Jesus has with him.

In the New Testament, the Spirit gives people God's view of things by forming them into a community that becomes Christ, pointing to Jesus Christ and through him to the Father. This transformation takes place at an ongoing personal and communal level. It is facilitated and empowered by personal openness to the Spirit and the personal relationship with each person of the Trinity. The Holy Spirit, therefore, inherently draws people into the triune divine community and into an authentic relationship with all the persons of the Trinity.

---

17. See Markey, *Who Is God?*, 92–98.

The theology of the Holy Spirit (called *pneumatology*) fundamentally deals with the interrelationships between the persons[18] of the triune community (the *Godhead*) and the relationships between individuals, between individuals and communities, and between communities and the divine community. In this sense, pneumatology is always relational and always implies some kind of interpersonal relationship. Regarding individual human beings, pneumatology is the connection between the Trinity's (and the persons of the Trinity) relationship with each person, which means there is a distinctive and unique way in which every person relates to the divine life and the divine plan.

Theological Challenges in the Development of an Adequate Pneumatology

This unique theological vision has not always been well-articulated in the theological tradition of Western Catholic Christianity.[19] There are many reasons for this. In the patristic period,[20] the focus of theological investigation was the existence of the Trinity itself and the unique identity of Jesus. Because most Christian thinkers identified the term *Logos* (an important concept in Hellenistic philosophy) with Jesus as the *Word* of God (John 1:1–18), they tended to envision the relationship between the Father and the Son as being like the relationship between the speaker and the word spoken: distinct but inseparable. This metaphor of human speech helped the early Christians explain to Hellenistic Romans how Jesus could be truly human and divine in the same way that the Logos (Word) of the Father would still share in the Father's divine nature. This theological process became the cornerstone of Christian theology in the early church and eventually yielded the development of the creed at the council of Nicea and the doctrinal formula of the two natures in the one person of Jesus at the Council of Chalcedon.[21]

In this interpretation of the relationship between the Father and the Son, the source and its Word, the role of the Holy Spirit as the Third Person was often unclear.[22] It was assumed the Holy Spirit was the link—the bond of love

---

18. There are fundamental differences between the patristic notion of "person" and a modern, Freudian sense of the self with a uniquely defined ego and individual center of consciousness. For more on this development, see Catherine Mowry LaCugna, *God for Us: The Trinity and Christian Life* (San Francisco: Harper, 1973), 243–317.

19. See Elizabeth A. Johnson, *She Who Is: The Mystery of God in Feminist Theological Discourse* (New York: Crossroad, 1992), 128–31.

20. Markey, *Who Is God?*, 35–46.

21. See Gerald O'Collins, *Christology: A Biblical, Historical, and Systematic Study of Jesus* (Oxford: Oxford University Press, 1995), 184–201, and Luke Timothy Johnson, *The Creed: What Christians Believe and Why It Matters* (New York: Doubleday, 2003), 216–53.

22. See Gelpi, *The Divine Mother*, 60–62.

and unity—between the Father and the Son that allowed them to be both distinct from one another, but also to share a common "mind" and "heart." The Spirit as the necessary unifying link between the Father and the Son implies the Spirit's role is that of unifying through mutual love the triune life of God. This internal role for the Spirit also conveys the Spirit's external mission to the world. The Spirit unifies or connects the divine community (God) with individuals, individuals with one another, and all together in the ultimate plan of God called the reign of God. The Holy Spirit, then, works the same way in human beings that it works in the internal life of God: it is the mind of God, as Paul insists (Rom. 8:9–17; 1 Cor. 2:10–16), which illumines persons to the profound love of God and points them to the concrete expression of this divine love in the Incarnation of Jesus Christ, who reveals to them the plan of the Father for all of creation.[23] To take on this mind of Christ, then, is to take on the mind of God and to begin not only "seeing" the world in a new way but also acting already as a person living in the coming reign of God.

Early Christian thought, however, tended to reduce the role of the Spirit to being simply the bond of love between the Father and Son, God and humanity, and thereby to overidentify the "mind" of God with the Son as Logos.[24] This tendency reduced the language of the New Testament and the vivid imagery of the divine *ruah* from the Jewish Scriptures, which often portrays the Spirit as the "wisdom" of God bestowed on persons. As has been demonstrated, there was no real need to separate the wisdom of God from the love of God, nor the mind of God from the heart, in describing the life of the Trinity. Nevertheless, this tendency occurred early in Western thought and became the dominate mode of portraying the identity and missions of the divine persons in the work of Augustine (354–430).[25] By identifying the Spirit as exclusively the bond of love between the Father and the Son and the mission of the Spirit as filling believers with the love of God and inspiring within them love for one another, the more constructive role of the Spirit was lost. It also unintentionally diminished the role of the Spirit to being merely the "link" or bond between the Father and the Son, and thus made it difficult for human beings to envision the Spirit as a unique person with a specific, very personal experience in their lives. Theologically, the Spirit has often been overlooked, neglected, or relegated to a secondary role in Trinitarian discussion and rarely treated separately as a focus of study like the Father and Jesus Christ. This has had serious repercussions, because the lack of Spirit-consciousness in the West has led to a type of theology that has lost focus on personal transformation and the triadic action of God in the New

---

23. Ibid., 59–65.
24. Ibid.
25. Ibid., 62–63.

Testament. The reduction of the Spirit to a feeling of love also makes it hard to understand the important work that the Spirit does in guiding and leading the community of disciples—the church—in their mission to take on the mind of Christ and cooperate with the Father's plan to bring the world to its fulfillment (Rom. 8; 1 Cor. 2:10).

The Roman Catholic Recovery of the Theology of the Holy Spirit in the Twentieth Century

After the Protestant Reformation, Western theologians in general and Roman Catholic theologians in particular tended to focus narrowly on areas of dispute between the churches and on a kind of defensive justification for the superiority of their own denomination. In the late eighteenth and early nineteenth century, however, a renewed, less defensive, interest in theology began to emerge in some Catholic universities. One of the most distinguished theologians from this period was Johann Adam Möhler (1796–1838).[26] Möhler was profoundly interested in writing a treatise on the church that integrated the theology of the New Testament and patristic periods with new understandings of history and philosophy. In 1825, Möhler produced a remarkable and important book entitled the *Unity of the Church*.[27] For Möhler, the starting point of any theology of the church had to be sustained reflection on the Holy Spirit.

Möhler believed Scripture and the tradition attest that the Spirit serves as the organizing and guiding principle of the church. Before this time, too many of the books on the church focused too narrowly on institutions, offices, and laws. Möhler insisted the Holy Spirit constituted the fundamental and dynamic principle underlying the structures, offices, and ministry of the church.[28] Möhler, drawing on the insight of Paul, described the church fundamentally as the body of Christ (Rom. 12; 1 Cor. 12). For Möhler, this implied the church is similar to a living, breathing organism that grows, changes, and develops over time.[29] It also implies the body of the church, like a human body, has a soul that animates and underlies it. For Möhler, the Holy Spirit acts as the "soul" of the church. This soul manifests itself in the visible and external organizational structures of the church. Möhler revived in the Roman Catholic Church theological interest in the person and action of the Spirit and the attempt to articulate the Spirit's presence in and connection to the life of the church. The twentieth century would see a radically renewed interest in both these areas.

---

26. Markey, *Creating Communion*, 35–37. See Michael J. Himes, *Ongoing Incarnation: Johann Adam Möhler and the Beginnings of Modern Ecclesiology* (New York: Crossroad, 1997).

27. J. A. Möhler, *Die Einheit in der Kirche* (Cologne and Olten: Hegner, 1956, originally published in 1825).

28. Ibid., 35.

29. Ibid., 36.

> ## Reflect and Discuss
>
> Consider how the power of beauty also serves as an underlying dynamic principle in the world of *Beauty and the Beast*. Beauty also tends to animate and change everything it encounters.

The mid-twentieth century saw a fascinating movement in Roman Catholic theology focused on the recovery and critical interpretation of the historical theological texts and treatises of the early and medieval periods of the church. This effort was joined with an even earlier Catholic recovery of scripture studies to create a dynamic moment of theological reflection and growth that culminated in Vatican II.[30] At the heart of this recovery movement, called *ressourcement* in French (the return to the sources), was the French Catholic theologian Yves Congar (1904–1995). Congar, like Möhler, set out to write an extensive theological treatise on the church. He was profoundly influenced by Möhler in the possibility and direction of this project. Like Möhler, Congar wanted to develop a vision of the church that was more vital than a mere explanation of the organizational structures and external elements. Congar was particularly interested in recovering the communal (rather than merely institutional or organizational) foundation of the church and its theological grounding in a renewed theology of the Holy Spirit.[31]

In a series of books in the 1950s, Congar began to envision the church as an expression of an essentially "Trinitarian plan."[32] In this Trinitarian plan, the Spirit makes Jesus' life and message continually present by enlivening and empowering the Christian community to represent this revelation to people in the contemporary world. The Spirit, responding to the plan of the Father that is revealed in Jesus Christ, animates the church as the body of Christ to continue his saving message and work in the world. The Spirit works to unite the church with Christ and the individual members with one another and their divine life in God.

Congar discovered that this "Trinitarian plan" is not at odds with the tradition but expresses its deepest articulation. He also realized the need to recover and more fully explore the reality and work of the Holy Spirit as the foundation and source of the life of the church. This desire to understand the Spirit became the focus of the second half of his career.[33]

---

30. See the section in this chapter headed "The Holy Spirit at Vatican II."

31. Möhler, *Die Einheit in der Kirche*, 45.

32. Yves Congar, *The Mystery of the Church*, trans. A. V. Littlefield (Baltimore: Helicon, 1960); Markey, *Creating Communion*, 46–47.

33. Ibid., 46–48; Yves Congar, "My Path-Findings in the Theology of the Laity and Ministry," *The Jurist* 32, no. 2 (1972): 169–88; Richard McBrien, "Church and Ministry: The Achievement of Yves Congar," *Theological Digest* 32 (1985): 203–11; Elizabeth Teresa Groppe, *Yves Congar's Theology of the Holy Spirit*, American Academy of Religion Academy Series (Oxford: Oxford University Press, 2004).

The Holy Spirit at Vatican II

The Second Vatican Council (commonly called Vatican II) was the twenty-first ecumenical council of the Catholic Church and the second to be held at Saint Peter's Basilica in the Vatican City.[34] An ecumenical council is a gathering of the Catholic bishops from around the world with theologians and other experts to consider questions of doctrine and organization that affect the universal church. Vatican II was called mainly to discuss matters internal to the life of the Catholic Church and questions about the relationship of the church to the modern world, with other Christian churches, and even with other world religions. The Council realized no adequate interpretation of its life and mission could take place outside of God's life and plan for all of creation revealed in the missions of the Son and the Spirit. In other words, all of creation and the church itself could only be adequately understood in light of the outpouring of the triune divine love of the Father, Son, and Holy Spirit. This Trinitarian insight served as the starting point, context, and goal of all theological reflection and practical planning for matters internal and external to church life.[35]

One of the most significant documents to emerge from the Council was *The Dogmatic Constitution on the Church* (*Lumen Gentium*). Contrasting with most previous treatises on the church, the Council chose to begin their examination of the nature and mission of the church by reflecting on the mystery of God and God's gratuitous choice to share the divine life with humanity. The Council grounded the theology of the church in the triune life of God and the missions of the persons of the Trinity toward creation. Critical to this triune vision, and echoing the earlier insights of Möhler and Congar, was the centrality of the Holy Spirit to life of the church.

Lumen Gentium insisted that the Spirit unites this body of believers into a single unity of life, which becomes the body of Christ. As such, the kingdom inaugurated by Christ "is already present in mystery," growing visibly through the power of the Spirit in the church. The Spirit then, by dwelling in both the church and the hearts of all people, will fully accomplish the saving action, willed by the Father and begun by Jesus Christ, of reuniting all creation with God. "Hence the universal Church is seen to be 'a people brought into unity from the unity of the Father, the Son and the Holy Spirit'" (*Lumen Gentium* 4). This means the church, because it is united to the Spirit—which moves freely through every human life, culture, time, and place—is somehow united to and present in even those places where the physical structures and organization of the church are not present or only partially present. This sense of the "universalism" of the

---

34. Markey, *Who Is God?*, 78–81.
35. Markey, *Creating Communion*, 58–59.

Spirit helps explain the universal nature of the church[36] and the presence of God to those outside the visible structures of the church and Christianity.[37]

This understanding of the universalism of the church through the work of the Holy Spirit is brought to full expression in one of the other major constitutions, *The Pastoral Constitution on the Church in the Modern World* (*Gaudium et Spes*). This document insists humanity comprises a single human family that is profoundly interconnected and related, not just through sharing the same planet, but through the presence of the same Spirit (*Gaudium et Spes* 2). For this reason, the document insists the church and human history share the same destiny and therefore must enter into a sincere dialogue of mutual understanding and cooperation. Those inside and outside of the church ultimately share the same problems, issues, hopes, and fears, and must work together to realize their common goals and address their difficulties. This constitution insists the church, because of its awareness of the life of the Sprit living within it, must bear the burden of initiating and enabling this shared process of reconciliation and transformation. The rest of this document is devoted to initiating, articulating, and analyzing the present condition of humanity in the light of the gospel and the history of the church.

This dialogical process, made possible by a renewed understanding of pneumatology, is at the heart of not only the church but the universe. The document does not conclude its sustained engagement with contemporary problems with solutions and prescriptions that the "world" needs to adopt. Rather, it concludes with a profound call for love and unity among all people. This call to unity extends beyond the bounds of church membership and ultimately includes a call to universal unity of all religions, peoples, and cultures (*Gaudium et Spes* 83–85, 92). The documents advance a remarkable connection between the pneumatological and dialogical foundations of the church.

This call to unity inherently includes a call to justice and recognition of the full human dignity of every human person and every community of people that make up the world. The constitution insists that because of the unique presence of the Spirit within it and its explicit knowledge of the unity of all humankind, the church must always stand in solidarity with all human beings in all dimensions of their lives and serve as an advocate of their absolute dignity and importance to God. The church must insist that governments, social systems, economic structures, and cultural practices protect and promote the infinite dignity and value of each human life. It is the unique charism of the church to act as a sign and instrument of compassion to those who are poor, weak, and

---

36. The term *catholic* comes from a Greek word meaning "universal" or "the whole." See Daniel P. Horan, "'Catholic' Doesn't Mean What You Think It Does," Huffpost, October 20, 2012, *http://www.huffingtonpost.com/daniel-p-horan-ofm/catholic-doesnt-mean-what-you-think-it-means_b_1978768.html.*

37. Markey, *Creating Communion*, 65–66.

most vulnerable in the world. In this sense, the documents recover the scriptural understanding of the Spirit as reconciler, advocate, and sustainer of the solidarity of all humanity.[38] The documents, therefore, also provide a new and significant insight into the essential relationship between pneumatology and social justice.

Reflect and Discuss

Do you see some connection between the power of beauty in *Beauty and the Beast* and the significance of the L'Arche community in representing Christ to the world? What is the underlying principle or power of the L'Arche community that enables it to serve as such an important witness to the Gospels' depiction of Jesus Christ?

The Feminine Face of God

The emergence of feminism in the twentieth century made it clear the lives, perspectives, and characteristics of women were not only neglected but actively suppressed throughout the history of Western culture. This means not only have women been socially and politically oppressed, but their unique perspective and identity has been regularly excluded from the evaluation and articulation of the Christian theological tradition. This raises the question of what has been lost, left out, and unexplored in the Scriptures and tradition that needs to be newly investigated and illumined. The doctrine of the Trinity and particularly the theology of the Holy Spirit will greatly benefit from a newly invigorated analysis from a feminine perspective. The contemporary American theologian Elizabeth Johnson advocates just such a project in her important book *She Who Is: The Mystery of God in Feminist Theological Discourse.*

Johnson discovers not only the strong presence of feminine imagery, metaphors, and analogies for God in the Hebrew and Christian Scriptures but also the almost systematic ignoring of these resources in the Western theological tradition. She demonstrates how this diminishes the theological process and the Christian revelation it is meant to convey. The omission of feminine images of God and the divine life from theology leaves God with only masculine, patriarchal characteristics, in direct contradiction to the way God is portrayed in the Scriptures. The maternal, loving, caring, nurturing depiction of the God who is love is often lost in the tradition, whereas God represented as distant, angry, judgmental, and obscure is often the norm.[39] That God is only talked about

---

38. Ibid., 93.

39. See Elizabeth Johnson, *Quest for the Living God: Mapping Frontiers in the Theology of God* (New York: Continuum, 2008), 90–112.

using male metaphors (such as Father, Son, and King) and using male pronouns (he, him, and his) means most ordinary people can only conceive of and talk about God as a man, with traditional male traits and male imagery. If one exclusively imagines God as male, even the best possible male, one loses a vast dimension of the creative imagination with which humans may know, understand, and worship God.[40]

Johnson cautions, however, that one cannot exclusively claim some traits are feminine and others masculine, as members of both genders often exhibit the same traits.[41] Johnson insists God is neither male nor female and God reveals Godself in the case of the risen Christ and the Holy Spirit as embodying both genders. Paul, for instance, specifically claims the risen Christ is no longer male or female, but a community composed of both genders and all kinds of people (Gal. 3:28). Furthermore, the predominant imagery of the Spirit in Scripture is mixed: sometimes the Spirit is directly portrayed as Lady Wisdom and a loving mother, but other times the Spirit is portrayed in generic terms: a lawyer or advocate, a rushing wind, tongues of fire, living water and the breath of God, or a dove hovering over both creation and Jesus.[42] Johnson insists, therefore, that any recovery of the feminine dimension of divine imagery needs to challenge the overall masculine and patriarchal structure that controls even human imagination so that God's true identity is understood apart from any human structures of power, authority, or order.[43]

Nevertheless, Johnson affirms Yves Congar's observation that in Catholic imagination many of the functions of the Holy Spirit are displaced onto the pope, adoration of the Eucharist, or the Virgin Mary.[44] Johnson goes on to describe how much of the description of Mary's role mirrors roles the Scriptures ascribe to the Holy Spirit: Mary is called mediator between humans and God, consoler, counselor, helper, and guide. Mary is also often pictured as the link between ordinary people and Christ, and through Christ to the Father. The New Testament ascribes all these to the Spirit.[45] Johnson believes that a richer and more complete theology of the Holy Spirit would result from an explicit designation of feminine imagery.

Furthermore, the role of a feminine "face" for God enables ordinary Christians to more adequately "makes sense" of the Trinity, especially with a more careful use of differentiating pronouns—for instance, "he" and "his" when

---

40. See Rosemary Radford Ruether, *Sexism and God-Talk: Towards a Feminist Theology* (Boston: Beacon Press, 1983).

41. Johnson, *She Who Is*, 53–57.

42. See John 14:16–17, 26, 16:7; Acts 2:1–4; John 7:37–39; Mark 1:9–11. Also see Gelpi, *The Spirit in the World*, 1–66.

43. Ibid.

44. Ibid., 129, referring to Congar, *I Believe in the Holy Spirit*, 1:159–66.

45. See also Leonardo Boff, *The Maternal Face of God: The Feminine and Its Religious Expressions*, trans. Robert R. Barr and John W. Diercksmeier (San Francisco: Harper and Row, 1987).

discussing the mission or work of the Second Person of the Trinity, but also "she" and "hers" when referring to similar actions of the Third Person of the Trinity. The designation of a real face to the Third Person of the Trinity would also enable ordinary Christians to picture her and see her as having a personal identity and role in their spiritual and religious lives. The recovery of a feminine face to God could facilitate the recovery and renewal of the Spirit to the everyday consciousness of ordinary Christians.[46]

Reflect and Discuss

In the section discussing the character of Belle, actress Emma Watson is quoted as saying that Belle's superpower is empathy. In the light of the preceding discussion of the Holy Spirit, does this description makes sense to you? How can empathy be a "power"? How do empathy and compassion change and transform individual lives and the sociopolitical realities? Is there something unique or special about the feminine dimension of human experience that conveys or represents the power of empathy?

What Difference Does It Make?

The Holy Spirit acts as the fundamental and universal presence of God in the world and human lives. The primary mission of the Spirit is to "make contact" with human consciousness and enable the loving power of God to influence, heal, strengthen, and direct human hearts and minds to the action of God in their lives. The transformative power of the Spirit makes the first contact with human beings in this interaction, but humans must respond. Life for Christians is an ongoing process of God's offer and human response. God continually attempts to liberate and empower people to respond positively to the offer of love and grace, but, ultimately, human choice plays a part in the historical emergence of events. Life is a project. The choice for God is not once and for all; neither is it obvious or simple. Rather, each life is an ongoing and continual series of choices, opportunities, habits, and practices that either respond to God's offer or ignore and reject it. Each life is an emerging process that is created under the guidance and direction of the Holy Spirit, if one is willing. God exists in people to the degree each person wants God to exist in him or her. God wants to be an active partner in each life, guiding it toward the reign of God, but persons have to choose to accept this offer of divine presence and guidance. The Holy Spirit acts as the first contact and as the guiding force into a relationship with all the

---

46. See Gelpi, *The Divine Mother.*

persons of the Trinity and the Trinity as a whole. For Christians, this journey, which Paul termed life (literally "walk") in the Spirit (Rom. 8:1–4), serves as the highest form of human consciousness and experience.

The universe shares in an analogous journey. It too is involved in an ongoing and emerging process. The universe is God's project: it is in many ways a diffusion of God's own life. Romans 8 declares the whole of creation longs for the salvation of the children of God. The Holy Spirit strives not just to reunite each individual with the divine community, but to bring the entire universe back into the divine life in some kind of transformed and glorious way. The work of the Holy Spirit exceeds merely human personal dimensions of existence and is at work in all the dimensions of God's creation to unify and redeem it to the full scope of God's original plan for the universe.

Reflect and Discuss

How does Belle's relationship with the beast/prince have a wider impact on the rest of the characters in the story and even on the physical environment in which they live? Reflect on the power of beauty as described in *Beauty and the Beast* and the power of the Holy Spirit as understood by liberation and feminist theologians.

Review Questions

1. What are the three main meanings of the Old Testament Hebrew term *ruah*?
2. What three aspects define the functional relationship between Jesus and the *pneuma* in the writings of Paul?
3. According to Paul, what is the unique mission of the *pneuma* in the church and the world?
4. In Acts, what is the relationship between the Pentecost events and the life of the Christian community?
5. What role does the *paraklētos* play in the Gospel of John?
6. What is the role of the Holy Spirit in the mission of the Trinity to the world?
7. Theologically, what are some reasons why the doctrine of the Holy Spirit has tended to be neglected by Western Christianity?
8. What led to the recovery of pneumatology in the twentieth century?
9. What are some of the main issues feminism raises for a contemporary theology of the Holy Spirit?

Discussion Questions

1. Why do you suppose the Scriptures use a variety of terminologies to describe the reality of the Holy Spirit?
2. Compare and contrast the presentation of the Holy Spirit in Paul, Luke, and John.
3. What challenges are posed to the Christian understanding of the Trinity by the marginalization of the Holy Spirit in the West?
4. Why might Vatican II's renewed interest in the church be connected with a renewed interest in the Holy Spirit?
5. In what ways do feminine or maternal images of God conform to or challenge your views of God?
6. Do you agree with Johnson's critique of mostly masculine language about God? Why, or why not? How might contemporary conceptions of gender influence how we talk about and make sense of God?

Additional Resources

PRINT

Boff, Leonardo. *The Maternal Face of God: The Feminine and Its Religious Expressions*. San Francisco: Harper & Row, 1987.

Congar, Yves. *I Believe in the Holy Spirit*. 3 vols. New York: Seabury; London: G. Chapman, 1983.

———. "My Path-Findings in the Theology of the Laity and Ministry." *Jurist* 32, no. 2 (1972): 169–88.

———. *The Mystery of the Church*. Baltimore: Helicon, 1965.

Dunn, James D. G. *The Christ and The Spirit*. Vol. 2, *Pneumatology*. 2 vols. Edinburgh: T&T Clark, 1998.

Ellacuría, Ignacio, and Jon Sobrino, eds. *Mysterium Liberationis: Fundamental Concepts of Liberation Theology*. Maryknoll, NY: Orbis; North Blackburn, Victoria, Australia: CollinsDove, 1993.

Gelpi, Donald L. *The Divine Mother: A Trinitarian Theology of the Holy Spirit*. Lanham, MD: University Press of America, 1984.

———. *The Spirit in the World*. Wilmington, DE: Michael Glazier, 1988.

Groppe, Elizabeth Teresa. *Yves Congar's Theology of the Holy Spirit*. American Academy of Religion Academy Series. Oxford; New York: Oxford University Press, 2004.

Hawthorne, Gerald F. *Dictionary of Paul and His Letters*. Downer's Grove. IL: InterVarsity, 1993.

Himes, Michael J. *Ongoing Incarnation: Johann Adam Möhler and the Beginnings of Modern Ecclesiology*. New York: Crossroad, 1997.

Holmes, Christopher R. J. *The Holy Spirit*. New Studies in Dogmatics. Grand Rapids: Zondervan, 2015.

Horan, Daniel P. "'Catholic' Doesn't Mean What You Think It Does." Huffpost. October 20, 2012. *http://www.huffingtonpost.com/daniel-p-horan-ofm/catholic -doesnt-mean-what-you-think-it-means_b_1978768.html*.

Johnson, Elizabeth A. *Quest for the Living God: Mapping Frontiers in the Theology of God*. New York: Continuum, 2007.

———. *She Who Is: The Mystery of God in Feminist Theological Discourse*. New York: Crossroad, 1992.

Johnson, Luke Timothy. *The Writings of the New Testament*. 3rd ed. Minneapolis: Fortress, 2010.

Kaltner, John, and Steven L. McKenzie. *The Back Door Introduction to the Bible*. Winona, MN: Anselm Academic, 2012.

Lennan, Richard, and Nancy Pineda-Madrid, eds. *The Holy Spirit: Setting the World on Fire*. New York: Paulist Press, 2017.

Markey, John J. "Clarifying the Relationship between the Universal and the Particular Churches through the Philosophy of Josiah Royce." *Philosophy & Theology* 15, no. 2 (January 1, 2003): 299–320.

———. *Creating Communion: The Theology of the Constitutions of the Church*. Hyde Park, NY: New City, 2003.

———. *Moses in Pharaoh's House: A Liberation Spirituality for North America*. Winona, MN: Anselm Academic, 2014.

———. *Who Is God? Catholic Perspectives through the Ages*. Winona, MN: Anselm Academic, 2016.

McBrien, Richard. "Church and Ministry: The Achievement of Yves Congar." *Theology Digest* 32 (Fall 1985): 203–11.

Möhler, Johann Adam. *Die Einheit in der Kirche: Oder, Das Prinzip des Katholizismus dargestellt im Geiste der Kirchenväter der drei ersten Jahrhunderte*. Cologne: J. Hegner, 1956.

Mollenkott, Virginia Ramey. *The Divine Feminine: The Biblical Imagery of God as Female*. New York: Crossroad, 1984.

O'Collins, Gerald. *Christology: A Biblical, Historical, and Systematic Study of Jesus*. Oxford: Oxford University Press, 2009.

Ruether, Rosemary Radford. *Sexism and God-Talk: Toward a Feminist Theology.* Boston: Beacon, 1983.

Thomasson-Rosingh, Anne Claar. *Searching for the Holy Spirit: Feminist Theology and Traditional Doctrine.* London: Routledge, 2015.

OTHER MEDIA

Barron, Bishop Robert. YouTube channel. *https://www.youtube.com/user/wordon firevideo.* See especially "Bishop Barron on the Holy Spirit."

Goergen, Donald, OP. *The Spirit of Life: A Catholic Retreat with the Holy Spirit.* DVD, CD, and MP3 file. Now You Know Media, 2017. Lectures by Donald Goergen, OP.

Conclusion

What Difference Does It Make?

God is love. For Christians, this is the most fundamental reality about God and describes both the way God is in Godself and the way God acts toward the whole of creation. God's love reaches, includes, and affects every person, the whole earth, and the entire cosmos. Whether human beings know and accept this reality does not change it. Love exists at the heart of the universe and shapes and forms every aspect of physical reality.

In the New Testament and the subsequent theological tradition, Christian thinkers go to great lengths to explain, understand, and interpret how Jesus and the Spirit proclaim and clarify the fundamental claim of their faith in God. Why? What difference does it make if Jesus really existed or is only a myth or story? What difference does it make if Jesus was really human or really divine or both or neither? Why do Christians care if the *ruah* of God described in the Hebrew Scripture is the same as the *pneuma* present in the New Testament narrative? How does the Spirit's relationship with the Father and the Son make any difference to the belief and destiny of Christian believers? What difference does the Spirit make to nonbelievers?

While this conclusion cannot hope to offer an extensive assessment of the whole tradition of theology about Jesus Christ and the Holy Spirit, it offers some insights on the significance of this process. Below are not merely conclusions but suggestions as to the implications of Christian belief about the mission of Jesus Christ and the Holy Spirit as revealed in the New Testament and reflected upon by the Christian community over the last two thousand years.

New Testament Christology: Who Is Jesus and Why Does It Matter?

For Christians, Jesus and his "nature," as the tradition comes to interpret it, make a difference to human beings in at least three ways.

Jesus Is Fully Human

The Gospels and epistles assume and even insist on Jesus' humanity. While Paul and the other epistle writers seldom refer to Jesus' life and historical ministry, they take for granted that these were known to the Christian communities to which they wrote and that these realities were confirmed by the Resurrection. From the infancy narratives through his life and ministry, the Gospels constantly portray Jesus as a real human person who grows, changes, and develops over time like everyone else. Jesus endures temptations and suffers from loss, misunderstanding, and his own limitations of time and place. He also experiences joy and seems to take genuine delight in normal human experiences like sharing a meal, being with friends, and helping those who are in need. The Gospel writers also consistently portray him as a devout Jew who remained faithful to this religious tradition for his whole life.

The Gospels agree, then, that whatever is divine about Jesus emerges from and is visible in his life and actions. It was through his life that his hearers in Jerusalem and the early Christians had to understand his identity. Indeed, the entire purpose of the Incarnation (taking flesh and pitching his tent among us) of the Son of God in the New Testament is so human beings can come to God and share in God's own life through witnessing it and imitating it in a human being like themselves. God, in Jesus, becomes a human being so human beings can participate in God's own life and eventually share in this divine life for eternity.

Jesus Dies

Like many of the Jewish prophets before him, Jesus' destiny is one of public failure and death.[1] Jesus is eventually arrested and tried by both the dominant

---

1. See Matt. 5:11–12, Mark 6:1–6, Luke 11:45–52, and John 3:13–16. The suffering of the prophets in the Old Testament served as a symbol for the relationship between God and Israel. Whenever the Jewish people failed to uphold the covenant, God would send a prophet to point out the sins of the people and warn of impending punishments. When the people rejected and condemned these prophets, they were symbolically rejecting God. Jesus' suffering on the cross at the hands of his own people mirrors this pattern. For more on the role of the Old Testament prophets, see Walter Brueggemann, *Old Testament Theology: An Introduction*, Library of Biblical Theology (Nashville: Abingdon, 2008), and Donald E. Gowan, *Theology of the Prophetic Books*, 1st ed. (Louisville: Westminster John Knox, 1998).

religious institution in his society and the government of the Roman Empire. What are the charges they bring against him? Some are superficially false, such as the claim that Jesus advocated destroying the Jewish Temple. Some are ambiguous, such as the assertion that he claimed to be the king of the Jews. Some are mysterious, such as Jesus' identification with the Son of Man coming on the clouds. All the charges do seem to have their roots in Jesus' sovereign teaching of God's plan and judgment on the institutions of this world. Jesus is the representative of God's kingdom (and, in that sense, king of the Jews), and he presents himself as someone who is more than just another prophet, someone who has the fullness of the Spirit in a unique way.

Jesus remains silent at his trial and refuses to offer a defense, perhaps because the charges say both too little and too much about his identity, and he knows his destiny flows out of his uncompromising preaching of the reign of God. Jesus' life unfolds because of the choices he makes to place himself on the side of the weak and vulnerable to insist that institutions (even religions) are here to serve people, especially the poor and those most in need. Jesus' trial and execution are the consequence of his actions and choices. They also serve as a special sign and event for Christians. To these Christians, Jesus' death represents the free choice of Jesus to live a life that leads, through its honesty about the reign of God, to violent conflict with self-seeking institutions and people. In this sense, Jesus' death is the ultimate example of the struggle between light and darkness, God's presence struggling with human sinfulness on earth and in human history. All human beings in the uniqueness of their own lives participate in this struggle of light versus darkness; hope versus despair; goodness, justice, and love versus constant patterns of violence, betrayal, and injustice.

For Saint Paul, the manner of Jesus' death is particularly significant, because he was not assassinated or killed by a mob but publicly and *legally* tried and found guilty by the religious and civil leadership in Jerusalem. For Paul, both the civil law and the sacred law were meant to protect the weak, promote justice, and guide people in the ways of truth. If the law was incapable of recognizing God's own presence in Jesus, but in fact put him to death, then the law was incapable of saving or helping human beings to find God and live righteously.[2] Paul declares that the death of Jesus signals not only the death to the law but death to all types of institutions claiming ultimate control over or obedience from human beings. For Paul, Jesus' death begins a new era of freedom, beginning with freedom from death itself and the power it has over human hopes and enterprises. By faith, humans are united to the Resurrection and so are given new life and God's Spirit in a complete and powerful way (Rom. 5:1–11). Furthermore, Jesus' death frees people not only from the power of death but from enslavement to false righteousness, represented by human institutions that

---

2. See Rom. 6–7; 2 Cor. 5:16–6:1.

claim ultimate authority but are in fact empty and false. Jesus' death frees human beings to live for God alone and unites them with God in a way that empowers them to give their lives entirely in service to others (Gal. 5:13–26).

Jesus Rises from the Dead

The early Christians were convinced Jesus' destiny did not end with the grave. This was an unusual conviction; while humanity and religion had always included room for ghosts, heavens, or survival after death, the Resurrection was extraordinary. The four Gospels present the Resurrection in different ways, and different groups of people see Jesus at different times: sometimes he walks through walls and locked doors, sometimes he is cooking fish on a beach inviting the disciples to breakfast, other times he must find and "recall" disciples who betrayed him, wandered away, or just returned to their previous lives. Without going into any detail, the Gospels locate the Resurrection of Jesus between, on the one hand, the resuscitation or quick revival of a corpse or a near-dead corpse into ordinary human life and, on the other hand, the survival of an inspiring idea or cause.

With the Resurrection, Jesus as a human being enters the future reign of God.[3] This means he comes to exist in a new kind of space, time, matter, and individuality. He does this because he shares or already participates not only in God's life but also precisely as a human being like every other human being. All human beings die. But in Jesus' Resurrection, a human person who literally bears the scars of this life in his body (John 20:26–28) returns from beyond death, indicating the triumphant future of God's plan for all human beings. The Resurrection, as the center of the paschal mystery, is not the act of a God in human clothing; in the Resurrection of the human being Jesus, God is seen to be especially present in this new and dynamic act of salvation from death and victory over chaos.

For Saint Paul, the Resurrection is the central event around which Christian faith revolves, for if Christ has not risen then Christian faith is in vain (1 Cor. 15:12–19).[4] Furthermore, Paul discerns three significant implications of Jesus' Resurrection. First, it implies hope for eternal life for the whole human race, because one human being has been raised from the dead proves the (future) general resurrection of the dead is real. Jesus has simply experienced the resurrection before the fact; he is the "firstfruits" of the resurrection of all people that will occur on the last day (1 Cor. 15:20–23). Second, this hope extends not only to Christians or even to human beings but to all creation

---

3. For more on death and the afterlife in this context, see Claudia Setzer, *Resurrection of the Body in Early Judaism and Early Christianity: Doctrine, Community and Self-Definition* (Leiden, Netherlands: Brill, 2004).

4. See also Rom. 8.

(Rom. 8:18–27).[5] Third, Jesus' outpouring of the Holy Spirit on all creation through the Resurrection means people can begin experiencing this future relationship with God right now in their daily lives—it is not simply a future possibility. This dimension of the paschal mystery will shape the Christian understanding of the purpose of the church, the sacraments, and the whole of the Christian life.

Assessing the Christological Tradition: How and Why Does God Become Human and What Difference Does It Make to Human Beings?

Revelation

Jesus reveals something about God and about humanity that could not otherwise be known. Jesus reveals God not only acts lovingly toward humans, but is love itself. The cosmos is not just a random, meaningless event, but is actually intended by God as an outpouring of God's love and a desire to share the internal love between the Father, Son, and Spirit with something outside of itself.

Furthermore, Jesus comes not merely as a messenger from this divine life but actually shares in it and demonstrates the extent to which God loves human beings. By desiring to become part of their lives—to pitch his tent with them—God chooses to enter into the human condition and directly experience human life with all of its joy, sorrow, tedium, difficulties, good, and evil. Jesus reveals that God does not simply create the world and walk away, leaving it to chance or to "battle it out" between competing human institutions or forces.

Jesus announces God's plan for human beings and also provides a direct and living example of that plan. He initiates a process that will bring about the ultimate triumph of that plan over the sorrows, tragedies, mistakes, and sinfulness of human history.

Jesus does more than tell people what God is like; Jesus shows people what God is like. That Jesus chooses again and again to place himself with the poor, oppressed, and outcast of his society over the religious, social, and economic institutional powers demonstrates God's choice and plan for human living. Furthermore, by dying unjustly and violently, Jesus demonstrates that human history has become terrible and that God is aware of this injustice and suffers along with all the victims of history. Jesus' Resurrection dramatically reveals God's response to the unjust and evil tide of history and the future destiny of all those human beings who are caught up in it. Jesus' Resurrection also reveals the future possibility that every human person could survive past death and be

---

5. See also 1 Cor. 15.

united to a new and different historical reality. Jesus' Resurrection also reveals the ultimate success of God's plan for the world over all odds and the seeming power of evil to control any particular moment in human history or a particular human life.

Transformation

The revelation Jesus provides transforms human self-understanding and changes people who accept it. Jesus' life and message enable faith, a personal relationship with God the triune community of persons. Faith in the God who is love and in Jesus Christ and his Resurrection gives hope that each life matters and that all humanity will participate in a life beyond death. This hope frees people from fear and from moral and psychic paralysis, and propels them to share the love they have experienced with other people. Faith and hope enables one to love as Jesus did: to love all those in need, forgive those who inflict harm, and to love people outside of one's tribe, nation, religion, socioeconomic class, and race. This love even extends to one's enemies.

Empowerment

To be transformed by Christ enables one to see the plan of God and desire to live it out in one's daily life. The risen Christ's gift of the Holy Spirit (the Third Person of the Trinity) on all believers and on the whole world frees people from the negative effects of sin and evil and empowers them to live in the new world that faith and hope encourages them to imagine. The Spirit empowers believers to take on "the mind of Christ" (1 Cor. 2:16) and thereby imitate Jesus in their own actions and relationships. Those who become like Christ are empowered to participate in the reign of God—the divine life—in the present moment and in the particular circumstances of their lives. The transformed believer who has the mind of Christ experiences assurance that this participation will not end in death but in new and transformed life with God.

The Theology of the Holy Spirit: Who Is the Holy Spirit and Why Does It Matter?

New Testament Perspectives: Spirit as Source and Mediator

Jesus mediates the divine *pneuma* to his disciples, but after Jesus' death, Resurrection, and Ascension the *pneuma* mediates the risen Christ to the community that has become his body. The *pneuma* searches the mind of God and gives believers the mind of Christ. The *pneuma* therefore is the source of gracious enlightenment and knowledge of the truth that Jesus learned from the Father and, in turn, incarnated.

The *pneuma* marks the beginning of a new creation: a new life characterized by sharing in the triune life of the Father, Son, and *pneuma* in a "mutual indwelling." This new reality makes all things "new" (2 Cor. 5:17) and has social, moral, and cosmic consequences. There is an outpouring of the *pneuma* on all believers. The mutual sharing of the *pneuma* is what makes the community of believers into the body of Christ. The interdependent sharing of charismata creates the type of authentic community life that characterizes a Christian community.

The moral demands of communal living are the direct consequences of the *pneuma*'s transformative action: to live "in the newness of spirit" (Rom. 7:6) describes the type of radical personal sharing and openness to the gifts and needs of others that connotes complete trust in the loving care of the Father and the saving example of the Son's life and ministry.

The *pneuma* acts not only as the source of unity and sharing of gifts within each community but also as the bond uniting each particular community into the wider communion of communities that together make up the body of Christ. This communion of communities acts analogously to each particular community in that there exists a necessary and mutual sharing of gifts and needs; this sharing builds up and interrelates the communities so that they function like a body. The divine *pneuma* coordinates and sustains this interaction and unites the entire universal communion of communities with the divine life.

Empowering Presence

The Holy Spirit, therefore, acts as the fundamental and universal presence of God in the world and human lives. The primary mission of the Spirit is "to make contact" with human consciousness and to enable the loving power of God to influence, heal, strengthen, and direct human hearts and minds to the action of God in their lives. The transformative power of the Spirit makes the first contact with human beings in this interaction, but humans must respond. For Christians, life is an ongoing process of God's offer and human response. God continually attempts to liberate and empower people to respond positively to the offer of love and grace, but, ultimately, human choice plays a part in the historical emergence of events.

Counselor or Guide

Life, then, is a project. The choice for God is not once and for all. Neither is it obvious or simple. Rather, each life is an ongoing and continual series of choices, opportunities, habits, and practices that either respond to God's offer or ignore and reject it. Each life unfolds through a process guided by the Holy Spirit, if one desires this. God exists in people to the level that people want God to exist in them. God wants to be an active partner in each life, guiding it toward the reign of God, but persons have to choose to accept this offer of divine presence and guidance. The Holy Spirit acts as the first contact and as the force that guides the individual into a relationship with the Trinity as a whole. For Christians, this journey, which Saint Paul referred to as living in the Spirit (Rom. 8:1–4), serves as the highest form of human consciousness and experience.

The universe shares in an analogous journey. It too is involved in an ongoing and emerging process. The universe is God's project; it is in many ways a diffusion of God's own life. Paul declares that the whole of creation longs for the salvation of the children of God (Rom. 8:19). The Holy Spirit strives not just to reunite each person with the divine community but to bring the entire universe back into the divine life in a transformed and glorious way. The work of the Holy Spirit exceeds merely human personal dimensions of existence and is at work in all the dimensions of God's creation to unify and redeem it to the full scope of God's original plan.

Index

Note: An 'i,' 'n' or 's' following a page number indicates an illustration, footnote or a sidebar, respectively